The Art of Relational Supervision

The Art of Relational Supervision demonstrates the clinical implications of the relational approach when applied to supervision. Describing her philosophical and theoretical rationale for setting up relational supervision groups, Helena Hargaden's goal in supervision is to reveal the relational unconscious within the client–therapist relationship. Here, with chapters from members of these groups, the vitality of supervision is brought to life as the clinical implications of the therapist's internal world are highlighted by group members. The complexity of group dynamics is explored and psychotherapists show how this positively affects their work with clients and patients.

The main themes examined in the book are the:

- Bi-directionality of the relational unconscious
- Ubiquity of therapeutic enactments and ruptures
- Intuitive use of improvisation
- Co-creation of the intersubjective third – the analytic third
- Focus on mutuality and reciprocity

Filled with case study examples, *The Art of Relational Supervision* will give readers a deep insight into the complex dynamics which form an integral part of any supervision and discover how this type of relational approach strengthens the therapeutic relationship to bring about significant psychological change for the client. It will be an invaluable resource for psychotherapists, counsellors and psychologists.

Helena Hargaden, DPsych, MSc, BA (Hons), TSTA (Teaching and Supervising Transactional Analyst), is UKCP registered and a member of IARPP, EATA, and a co-founder of International Association of Relational Analysis. She has a private practice in West Sussex. In collaboration with others she began the relational developments in transactional analysis. She has been widely published and translated into a number of other languages.

The Art of Relational Supervision

Clinical Implications of the use of Self in Group Supervision

Edited by Helena Hargaden

Routledge
Taylor & Francis Group

LONDON AND NEW YORK

First published 2016
by Routledge
2 Park Square, Milton Park, Abingdon, Oxon OX14 4RN

and by Routledge
711 Third Avenue, New York, NY 10017

Routledge is an imprint of the Taylor & Francis Group, an informa business

© 2016 Helena Hargaden

British Library Cataloguing in Publication Data
A catalogue record for this book is available from the British Library

Library of Congress Cataloguing in Publication Data
The art of relational supervision : clinical implications of the use of self in group supervision / edited Helena Hargaden.
    pages   cm
Includes bibliographical references and index.
1. Psychotherapists–Supervision of.   2. Psychotherapy–Study and teaching–Supervision.   3. Physician and patient.   I. Hargaden, Helena.
RC459.A78 2016
616.89'140076–dc23
2015011650

ISBN: 978-1-138-83845-1 (hbk)
ISBN: 978-1-138-83846-8 (pbk)
ISBN: 978-1-315-72788-2 (ebk)

Typeset in Times
by Out of House Publishing

Printed and bound in Great Britain by Ashford Colour Press Ltd., Gosport.

Contents

Contributors

Helena Hargaden, DPsych, MSc, BA (Hons), TSTA (Teaching and Supervising Transactional Analyst), is UKCP registered and a member of IARPP, EATA. Helena is a psychotherapist, writer, coach, supervisor and consultant. In collaboration with others she developed relational perspectives of TA and has been widely published and translated into a number of other languages. She is co-founder of International Association of Relational Transactional Analysis (IARTA) and co-founder with Maya Jacobs-Wallfisch of the Transgenerational Trauma Forum, is an international speaker on relational psychotherapy and has a private practice in Sussex, UK.

Brian Fenton, Psych BSc (Hons), MSc Psychotherapy, Post-Graduate Diploma in Clinical Supervision, is a provisional training and supervising transactional analyst and UKCP-registered psychotherapist. He has a particular interest in the development of relational transactional analysis. Brian has a private therapy and supervision practice based in Whitstable in Kent, and can be reached at brianjfenton@yahoo.co.uk.

Heather Fowlie, MA, MSc Psychotherapy, teaching and supervising transactional analyst, Diploma in supervision, is UKCP registered. She is head of the TA department at the Metanoia Institute in London, works in private practice in Ewell as a psychotherapist and supervisor, and is particularly interested in integrating other models of psychotherapy, especially object relations within a relational approach to transactional analysis. She is a founder member of IARTA and has written several articles. She is co-editor with Charlotte Sills (2012) of *Relational Transactional Analysis: Principles into Practice* and is currently busy working on a second book, *Relational TA: A primer.*

Birgitta Heiller, PhD, MSc, TSTA, CTA, is a registered psychotherapist and counselling psychologist, and a past co-editor of the *Transactional Analysis Journal*. She maintains a private clinical and supervision practice in Guildford, UK. Her recent publications include 'Narcissism and TA', in the *Journal of the Institute of Transactional Analysis* (2004); 'Life Scripts: an existential perspective' (with Charlotte Sills), in *Life Scripts* (2010, edited by R. Erskine and published by Karnac); and 'Is relational transactional analysis terminable?', in *Relational Transactional Analysis* (2011, edited by Fowlie and Sills and published by Karnac).

Gina Sweeting, BSc, MSc, Diploma in Counselling, Diploma in Couples Counselling, Certificate in Supervision, trained as a Humanistic Integrative Counsellor at The Iron Mill Institute in Devon in 1999. Since then she has worked both privately and in the NHS undertaking long-term and short-term counselling. Her interests have included groups, trauma and motherhood, and she runs groups as part of her private practice in Sussex. She is a qualified couples therapist, having trained in couples therapy using the arts.

Jane Todd, BA, MSc, is a UKCP-registered provisional teaching and supervising transactional analyst, and runs a private psychotherapy and supervision practice in South West London. She trained at the Metanoia Institute in West London and has a particular interest in early developmental trauma and adult psychotherapy. Jane co-ran groups at The Priory for clients with eating disorders and has presented workshops using transactional analysis to help families and teenagers manage the teenage years. She currently co-runs workshops on sleep and insomnia, and is passionate about the process of supervision and its impact on both the clinician and client.

Marion Umney, MA, MSc, is a provisional teaching and supervising transactional analyst and a UKCP-registered psychotherapist. With an original background in business and management education, she currently has a private practice in East Sussex. Her previous publications have related to business and education and include: *Managing Health Service Information, Information for Control* and *Decision Making and Health and Social Service Management*, all commissioned and published by the Open Learning Foundation; and *Evaluation of Joint Posts and New Roles to Support Learning in Practice for Pre-registration Nursing and Midwifery Students* and *The Impact of AP(E)L on Pre-registration Health Professional Education Within the Context of Modernisation*, both commissioned and published by the Department of Health.

Foreword

Professor Charlotte Sills

What a feast – of stories, of ideas, of theories and, most particularly, of people. On every page we hear the voice of someone, be it Helena, the author (both of the book and of the supervision group experience) or her contributors, who offer their stories and thoughts and experiences of being in relational supervision groups, so that the process comes alive.

The book not only explains, it demonstrates and illustrates what is meant by a relational approach to supervision, and indeed to psychotherapy. I hope it will be a useful response to that common question, 'But aren't we all relational?' Well yes, of course we are, if 'relational' is meant as 'in relationship' – shaping and being shaped at every moment of life from conception to death. In that sense, we are all relational. Experience is co-created to a greater or lesser extent. And therapists probably all agree that taking an interest in how relating is happening – a client's relating to self, to others and to the therapist – is a fruitful endeavour and worthy of exploration.

This book goes further. In Chapter 1, Helena overviews the development of the relational perspective in psychoanalysis and humanistic psychotherapy, and explores some of the psychological traditions that have both contributed to it and also, of course, been influenced by it. She examines some of the philosophical and theoretical lenses that have focused on the process of relating and then explores in depth an approach that is based in the realms of unconscious relationality, demanding that the therapist be ready to find the client inside herself (Bollas, 1987, p. 202). She describes the creation of a model of group supervision that mirrors the process of practice, in which practitioners take the risk of deeply exploring themselves and their own feelings, exposing them to the light of the 'third'. The 'third' is a major theme in the book, discussed by Helena and several of the contributors. It has many faces, but the common theme is the provision of a symbolic space in which the unconscious processes and meanings of the group members find resonance in each other; mind is brought to bear on inchoate experience; and nonverbal, non-conscious and unsymbolised material can be given new language. This space becomes the powerful heart of the group.

The book unfolds like a thrilling novel, as, within the framework of telling the story of the group life, each of the contributors illuminates the process through his or her own experience and the theoretical supports and meanings they have found useful. Just a few examples: Brian Fenton describes how he 'experienced intersubjectivity in action not only between self and other but also as scattered or fragmented elements of experience, gathered by the group participants from their subjective experience in response to my client presentations'; Heather Fowlie articulates the core principles of relational psychotherapy and its aim to bring 'a client's relational expectations into awareness, where they limit the capacity to be open, spontaneous and intimate'; Marion Umney focuses on the importance of narrative in therapy, quoting Mitchell (2002), who said that 'we are our stories, our accounts of what happened to us', thus 'no stories, no self' – and much more. It is striking how varied the chapters are, each a jewel in itself, each revealing its author's unique style of engaging with relational theory and integrating it into their personal therapeutic approach.

This book not only describes relational practice, and relational supervision in particular, it also demonstrates it, in its aliveness and co-created experience. It is full of wonderful vignettes of client work as well as touching accounts of the therapists' personal journeys.

It is important to add that Helena does not reject the ordinary tasks of supervision – the ethical or practical aspects. These are, of course, recognised even though it is an approach designed for more advanced practitioners, where the need for the formative or normative tasks in supervision (Proctor, 1988) is less. However, the book will appeal to practitioners at any level. The 'beginning therapist' will also gain much from reading about and recognising their own vulnerabilities in the shared experiences of senior practitioners. This can sit alongside their more formal learning, allowing and inviting another dimension of understanding.

Acknowledgements

Many thanks and much appreciation to all who contributed to the making of this book.

A warm acknowledgement to the contributors and current members of the relational supervision group who have generously shared their ideas and reflections on relational supervision. Special thanks to Jane Todd (see Introduction), as well as to Joan Dallas, Brian Fenton, Fari Ghaemrasekh, Cate Masheder, Kareen Ryden, Gina Sweeting and Marion Umney for reading scripts and offering valuable feedback.

My gratitude to Carole Shadbolt, who was so crucial in offering me encouragement and informed feedback, in the early part of writing and putting this book together.

I would like to recognise Suzanne Boyd and Misha Douglas for your generous interest and creative responses and Enid Welford for your edits and challenges, expressed with warmth and humour.

Appreciation to my friends and colleagues Charlotte Sills and Keith Tudor for their finessed editing skills, and their very valuable feedback, and to Andrew Samuels, who offered encouragement and valuable thoughts.

A special heartfelt thank you to all clients, patients and supervisees for continuing to teach us so much.

Introduction

The aim of this book is to describe a relational approach to supervision by putting it in the context of experiential learning. It is is based on the premise that play, use of the imagination, intuition and improvisation will inform and enhance the clinical work in supervision. In 2002 I started a journey to explore what the territory of relational supervision might look like. I formed a number of supervision groups, all composed of senior trainees or qualified practitioners who were willing to experiment with a particular form of engagement with each other and with the client material. Over the months and years, we explored and developed the model, refining our approach and recording its impact. This book describes the journey.

This way of working is variously described and debated by six psychotherapists in lively narratives in which they describe their experience in relational supervision groups. In their accounts they bring us into their inner worlds to explore what the method tells them about their therapeutic work, and offer their analysis of how this process brings depth and meaning to their practice. I want to make a special acknowledgement of Jane Todd, a member of the relational supervision group, who prompted me to write and edit this book. She thought it would be useful and even inspirational for other clinicians to learn about this relational approach to supervision using the *self* of the supervisee. Without this prompt I doubt this book would exist!

The underlying philosophy for this relational approach to supervision, described in detail in Chapter 1, is that we do not help people with theory, but with our selves. It is our personal relational abilities for emotional engagement, discernment, nuanced attunement and perhaps most of all our integrity that will inform how we work with people who are suffering, as well as how we engage with relational theories. Thus theory becomes secondary to the human exchange. That said, the freedom to improvise in this way is predicated on the creation of a structured and contained space that allows for an ongoing dialectic between experience and relational theorising. It is

of course incumbent upon us as professionals to refine our clinical sensibilities by increasing our theoretical diversity, which may be ancient wisdoms
or existing theories from different modalities. The use of theory, metaphors
and life experience deepens our understanding of the many nuanced ways in
which we pay attention to our own experience.

This way of working is not only a reflection of me, though. It has emerged
through a meeting of the collective minds of me and members of the relational
supervision groups I have worked with over the years. This way of thinking
about supervision emphasises the use of group culture and dynamics in order
to co-create a space for *the meeting of minds*, opening up the space for *mutuality and reciprocity* in the service of finding the client in the therapist; the
possibility for plurality of meaning-making in which the vulnerability of both
therapist and client is explored and in which the *intuitive self* of the therapist
is encouraged; the *involvement of the group in enactments* and to take time to
find the meaning and the implications for the clinical work. This process is
brought vividly alive by Heather Fowlie in Chapter 3, where she focuses on a
single presentation in a relational supervision group and the intense dynamics
that changed her emotionally. She demonstrates clearly how this affected her
clinical work in a positive way. A thoughtful perspective on her involvement
in group dynamics is described in Chapter 5 by Gina Sweeting, who shows
how a *meeting of minds* in group supervision altered her thinking and behaviour as a clinician.

Towards an understanding of relational supervision

There are many excellent books on supervision written by supervisors whose
wisdom and expertise has supported the theoretical development of this most
interesting and challenging profession. In particular Hawkins and Shohet
(1989) set the bar high with their clear and creative exposition of parallel process, in which they demonstrate how the dynamics between therapist and client or patient can be recreated in supervision. This has been of immense value
to all trainee supervisees and well-established supervisors who unwittingly
get entangled in unconscious communications. Carroll and Tholstrup's edited
book (2001) offers a contemporary view of integrative supervision in which
supervisors of whatever ilk can find informed and insightful ways to think
about the collaborative nature of the supervisory relationship. Closest to the
relational edge, which is the focus of this book, is the work of Frawley-O'Dea
and Sarnat (2001), whose immensely knowledgeable work takes us from
the traditions of psychoanalytic supervision into the heart of the relational

approach, describing some of the challenges and the joys of working at the interface of relational unconscious processes. I related to their observation that supervisory theory had not kept up with the evolution of clinical theory, but in this book my goal is not so much to offer theories of supervision, as to contextualise supervision in the framework of the most recent clinical developments in relational thinking. Ogden (2005), in his article on analytic supervision, is nearest in form to what I am creating here, describing how important it is for the supervisor to provide a space in which the supervisee is enabled to 'dream', as a way of discovering emotional truths about the clinical work. The move from more traditional methods of supervision towards a relational approach is described by Marion Umney in Chapter 7 in her personal account of her experience in the group and then with a young female client. In a moving and beautifully clear style she takes us through her process of change from cognitive-based therapy to a more reflective symbolic process.

Background to relational theory

I have suggested elsewhere (Hargaden, 2014a) that the term 'relational' provides a symbol of integration, enabling clinicians of whatever modality to cross-fertilise with other theoretical perspectives and discover those which most closely mirror their clinical sensibilities. In this way, clinicians are released from a rigid interpretation of their own theoretical modality. Further, they can find contemporary evidence to recognise how elements of their original modality may have become theoretically insignificant, or even inaccurate, as with some obsolete theories of child development within transactional analysis, for example.

There is not a defined body of relational theory as such but the relational approach is more a philosophical attitude which at core involves us in a subjective engagement with ourselves and with our clients and patients. It is through the development of our relational philosophies and theories that the relational ethos develops. Nevertheless there are substantial works that have forged the path towards a deeper and broader relational understanding. For example Stern's (1985) collaborative scientific research over thirty years captured the complex and fascinating interpersonal world of the infant, obliging clinicians, of whatever ilk, to engage anew with the complexity, mystery and subtlety of the development of subjective experience. By demonstrating the scientific basis for an innate predisposition towards intersubjectivity (this term is described and discussed in the ensuing chapters), Stern, alongside others (Beebe et al., 1992; Damasio, 1999; Schore, 1994) have demonstrated how the infant mind develops through the sharing of minds, shaped by affect (or the absence of it), gestures and intersubjective affective regulation. It is through this process that the unconscious mind of the (m)other is transferred to the infant. This evidence of the ubiquity of the bi-directional unconscious, which had previously been understood intuitively, has stimulated creative discussions on the co-created and co-creative nature of interconnectedness and implicit relational knowing (Yontef, 1988; Benjamin, 2007; Tudor and Summers, 2014). The relational approach has many different sources depending on your original theoretical perspective. In the humanistic tradition, along with other modalities, we think of Buber (1970/1923) as the originator of intersubjective thinking, with his philosophical perspective of I-thou: 'The actual other who meets me meets me in such a way that my soul comes in contact with his as with something that it is not and that it cannot become. My soul does not and cannot include the other, and yet can approach the other in this most real contact' (Buber, 1999, p. 6). Carl Rogers, Eric Berne and Fritz Perls, among others, also contributed to the idea that therapeutic relatedness involves a bilateral process of mutuality. These ideas were further developed by the substantial contributions of Mitchell (2000), Aron (1990) and Benjamin (2002a, 2002b), and many others in the relational psychoanalytic field, developments which are referred to throughout this book.

I think it important to make a distinction between the effect of the relational approach on humanistic and psychoanalytic traditions. For instance at a meta level the relational approach has involved a more intense focus on the depth of the intra-psychic and relational unconscious than was previously the case in the humanistic tradition. In the case of transactional analysis (TA), for example, which has sometimes been criticised as too reductive and schematic, relational perspectives created opportunities to go beyond the schemas and reconnect with object relational structures inherent in the foundational models of TA (Novellino and Moiso, 1990). A creative revision of TA theory made it compatible with Stern's schema of the domains of self (Hargaden and Sills 2002), providing broader and deeper theoretical possibilities for transactional analysts. Relational psychoanalysts on the other hand seem to have gone through a transformative process by discovering the power and potency of interpersonal relatedness and its connection to the relational unconscious. They offer perspectives which add increased layers of depth to our understanding of theories of mutuality, reciprocity and the co-created relationship (Aron, 1990; Benjamin, 2002a, 2002b).

The terms 'relational', 'relatedness' and 'the relationship' can however seem deceptively simple, whilst at the same time causing significant controversy over their meaning, a debate which is taken up by Birgitta Heiller in

Chapter 4. For those readers who are unsure or sceptical about the relational approach you will find some resonance and yet maybe also reassurance in Birgitta's reflections on her experience in a relational supervision group. Put simply, at its basic level of understanding, the relational approach requires us to think about how we meet each other and don't meet each other, and how we meet ourselves, always taking into account the fact that the unconscious dimension of experience will be greater and the most influential upon our behaviour. Such an intense process often brings with it feelings of shame, and in Chapter 8 I discuss the potentially destructive impact of this emotion, yet think it fundamentally important for us to engage with it. It is an inevitable part of the intensity involved in finding the client and patient within ourselves.

Relational supervision

I began my journey in relational supervision by wondering how to make the relational ideas I had been developing in collaboration with other colleagues more central to the supervisory process. In particular, relational thinking (influenced by neuroscientific studies) has advanced our knowledge of the nature of trauma, a common theme in our work, alongside the accompanying defensive process of dissociation. How to work relationally, given the clinical complexities of working with dissociative processes, is succinctly captured by Bollas: 'in order to find the patient we must look for him within ourselves' (1987, p. 202). The question this book engages with is how to find the dissociated aspects of the patient in the therapist through the supervisory process. Working at this level requires us to engage with signs, symbols and metaphors, a particularly fine example of which you will find in Chapter 6, where Jane Todd draws on her associations with the story of *Alice in Wonderland*. In an informed and intense account of her struggle to protect herself and the therapy from negative patriarchal influences, Jane reflects on the positive use of feminine power in the therapeutic relationship.

From a humanistic perspective we here concentrate on the relational unconscious, mindful that the unconscious will only reveal itself through 'peculiar effects' (Meier, 1995, p. 13). The relational approach to supervision described in Chapter 1 and referred to throughout the book reflects my theoretical interests, my sensibility and the co-created way in which I work. In this book you will find intense and dialectical demonstrations of core relational concepts, such as the nature of mutuality and reciprocity; the bi-directional nature of the relational unconscious; the co-construction of experience; the role of ruptures and enactment; and the use of 'thirds' as a move away from binary thinking. Through vivid personal accounts these concepts take on a life outside of the more usual domain of academic study, challenging the reader to involve themselves in the paradox of the subjective experience of the writer. In Chapter 2, for example, Brian Fenton offers a well-researched perspective on the nature of intersubjectivity, integrating his discourse with personal experiences that are as insightful as they are revealing of his vulnerability. Overall my purpose is to co-create, with the reader, an opportunity for reflection on their own experience and practice. As leader and initiator of several relational supervision groups, I have had many challenges which made me more conscious of my vulnerabilities, a process I share in Chapter 9. In that chapter I also offer an analysis of why this way of working is unsuitable for some therapists, make a distinction between the often misunderstood ideas of equality and mutuality, and consider some of the ethical and shadow sides of our profession.

Chapter 1

A relational approach to supervision

Helena Hargaden

This approach is founded on an understanding that most relatedness is unconscious, that the unconscious mind cannot be discovered through cognitive means, and is based on a humanistic interpretation of the bi-directionality of transference and counter-transference (Moiso, 1985; Moiso and Novellino, 2000; Hargaden and Sills, 2002). The relational approach has its roots in the humanistic philosophy of a dialogic relatedness (Buber, 1970/1923), in which the therapist's use of self and willingness to be vulnerable and change in relationship, is considered paramount to effective therapy with suffering people. There is an emphasis upon containment, with an understanding that the container will need to crack (ruptures and enactments) to shine a light on dissociated material. Drawing on theories of intersubjectivity and the co-created 'third', definitions of which will be found below and throughout the chapters in this book, this relational approach has been co-created between supervisor and many supervisees who have been willing to travel on an experiential relational journey of discovery about how and why relationship and relatedness matters. It is primarily for this reason that I refer to relational supervision as an art form.

Interest in relational psychotherapy has been developing over many years, both in the psychoanalytic field (Mitchell and Aron, 1999; Aron and Benjamin, 1999; Aron, 2006) and in the humanistic tradition (Yontef, 1988; Shmukler, 1991; Moiso, 1985; Hargaden and Sills, 2002). Research (Asay and Lambert 1999; Beutler and Harwood, 2002; Luborsky and Auerbach, 1985) indicates that the relationship is a central feature of effective outcomes in psychotherapy. Before I discuss some major influences on my relational approach I begin with a reflective analysis of my experience of supervision practice.

Pitfalls in supervision: power and ethics

In the following section I offer my critique of some supervisory practices, not from a position of superiority, but more from the perspective of how we may learn from our experience and our mistakes. The question I am interested in here is what really works and supports our clinical practice and what is either unhelpful or damaging. Perhaps it is as a supervisee that we are best positioned to critique the process of supervision since the supervisee is best positioned to know what has been clinically fruitful in the therapeutic relationship. It is therefore from my experience as a supervisee that I offer the following reflections.

I have had many enlightening experiences which have informed my work as a therapist and as a supervisor. I feel gratitude towards those supervisors I have had in the past thirty years who have been willing to sit with me and listen, play and tussle with the questions, concerns and anxieties I brought to supervision. Acknowledging this positive experience however, and with the benefit of hindsight, I have reflected on those aspects that were either not so helpful or quite damaging. Beginning in the mid-1980s I struggled initially to know what I was supposed to do in supervision. In Chapter 4 Birgitta Heiller highlights the experience of the trainee psychotherapist and how, as supervisor, she manages the need for certainty and direction often thought to be typical of the new trainee in therapy. I was reminded of starting out in the profession as a trainee psychotherapist and new supervisee when I felt alienated by the behavioural focus and insistence on 'objectivity'. From this experience I learned how unhelpful it can be when a supervisor relies too heavily on formal structures that become so controlling that no illicit thought or feeling could possibly escape into the environment!

It was with some relief that I found a supervisor who also seemed interested in the feelings of the therapist, creating an environment it which it was more possible to deepen associations and relational connections between therapist and client. In hindsight I think though that within the humanistic tradition we have tended to elevate feelings. I have seen how this process can lead to gratuitous and unfocused dynamics that do not change anything. In this context I found reading Guggenbhul-Craig's (1971) critique of empathy useful, in which he suggests there is a shadow side to empathy that bestows an exaggerated and false sense of worth on the person expressing the feelings whilst simultaneously making the empathic person powerful, enabling them to hide their realness. An example of this is when the emotionality of a member of a supervision group is allowed to eclipse the clinical concerns of the client or patient. This way of working can seem to be 'relational' but often leaves other participants feeling hidebound to be 'empathic' with the emotional needs of another member of the group, quietly wondering, 'What about the client?' or more particularly, 'What about my client?'. Such an emphasis on 'empathy' can create an environment of 'faux love'. Nonetheless feelings of course are important, for without them 'the edifice of reason cannot operate properly' (Damasio, 1999, p. 43). The learning from this critique is that feelings used in this way are indeed the superhighway to the unconscious enabling us to refocus on the *meanings* inherent in feelings, that we are more likely to access different levels of unconscious associations through the emergence of new language (Eigen, 2006b).

Conversely, within the very different tradition of classical psychoanalytic supervision, I found that intellectual analysis seemed to trump feelings, that in essence feelings became second-class citizens. Although I found psychoanalytic supervision to be rich with insightful perspectives, there seemed to be an implicit expectation that the supervisor's intellect, knowledge and ability should be understood as superior to the therapist's knowledge, and that the analyst's interpretation was non-negotiable, regardless of what feelings might be in the room. Of course this may have changed over the years, and I do not wish to minimise the indisputable contribution of psychoanalysis to the development of the relational approach; for example, my most recent experience in psychoanalytic supervision has been very different in kind. I do not know if this is because that tradition is also changing or I just happened to meet an egalitarian-minded person with whom I had a supervisory relationship based entirely on mutual respect and reciprocity, providing an atmosphere in which I significantly increased my emotional and intellectual development as a clinician. Yet two examples come to mind of a particularly damaging effect of a non-relational, non-negotiable approach to supervision, and although they occurred in the psychoanalytic tradition they are not limited to that modality alone. More recently, for example, I hear not entirely dissimilar stories from trainees who are on placements, sometimes in environments that seem to be driven by anxiety, and rigid attitudes towards clinical work not confined to psychoanalysis but across all modalities. Some may recognise elements of their experience of the misuse and even abuse of power by people in organisations in the following two examples.

In the first example I was a trainee psychotherapist on a placement at a London psychiatric hospital. My psychoanalytic supervisor stopped my work with a young Irish woman, a victim of the troubles in Northern Ireland, because he considered that I worked too interpersonally: this was after I had made a strong feeling connection with her, as a result of which she experienced a breakthrough in her depression. Not only did he seem fearful of the interpersonal exchange that had developed between myself and the patient, he failed to understand the significance of the cultural complexity embedded in the therapeutic relationship I was engaged in with the patient (see below for a fuller discussion using the cultural 'third' as a symbol to examine what happened between the supervisor and me).

The supervisor became anxious at the type of intimacy that developed between myself and the patient, a closeness that was connected to our shared cultural connection; a connection that was forged through a shared affective experience of the effects of the Irish diaspora (I say more about this in Chapter 8). I knew this to be vital to her mental health because I shared a conviction along with Geertz (1973) and Samuels (1993) (see my collaboration too with Tudor in Tudor and Hargaden, 2002), that there is no such thing as human nature without culture. Instead, the supervisor viewed cultural analysis as irrelevant to the work of psychology and interpersonal connection as flawed and dangerous. I have often wondered about that young woman, and how she fared. The psychoanalyst was able to behave in this way because he came from a place of guaranteed superiority, supported by the hospital structures, a theoretical perspective that was rooted in quite a rigid methodology and a sense of his own certainty that he was absolutely right.

In a different and more benign example, in part because there was no organisational ballast behind the supervisor and, as you will see, the client's natural instinct was to reject what he experienced as an unhelpful interruption into the therapy relationship, a different psychoanalytic supervisor told me that my interpretation of my client's dream was facile, superficial and completely missing the mark. I had not mentioned that it had been my client's interpretation. The scornful tone of the supervisor unfortunately made it too difficult for me to integrate his understanding into my subjectivity. Instead, I offered the 'superior' interpretation to my client, who snorted and returned to his next session to tell me about a dream he had had in which a big fat farmer caused the plane in which my client and I were on a journey to crash into an empty field! I think this is a good example of how an interpretation, delivered in such a disembodied way, misses the relational point, and in doing so, not only loses the intended impact, but makes what might have been a useful clinical intervention redundant. Maybe the supervisor was accurate, maybe too I was so in awe of the supervisor I could not integrate his interpretation into my subjective experience, which brings me to several questions about ethics and supervisory authority. How do we own our authority in the relational field? Where does the balance lie between authority and relationality? The supervisor, by definition, has seniority and responsibility, so how can we maintain those boundaries as well as being truly co-productive? I say more about this in Chapter 9 when I give examples of how ethical questions can appear to conflict with the relational ethos when mutuality has been confused with equality.

As a supervisor of more than twenty-five years of course I have fallen into some of the above traps. Supervision is a complex and challenging job! Many questions arise about how to find a balance between empathy, cognition and the provision of a space in which some aspects of the unconscious of both the client and the therapist, as well as that of the supervisor, can reveal themselves.

Early influences on the development of my relational approach to supervision

Since the advent of the now obligatory supervision course there is quite an emphasis upon theories of supervision which, although very useful, may also suggest that there is a uniform way to do supervision. The question discussed here is how the *self* of the supervisor is formed and influenced, how she draws on her life experience, including her unique way of integrating theory into her practice, and why this matters in the clinical situation of supervision. In the following examples I share some of the influences upon my clinical development to demonstrate how our personal experiences and subjective integration of theories shape who we are as supervisors. I show how this will both consciously and unconsciously impact upon the type of supervisory environment we co-create with our supervisees.

Improvisation and intuition

In my younger years, working as an English and Drama teacher, I learned the art of improvisation. Improvisation is defined as being able to 'make or contrive without preparation in an emergency' (Chambers, p. 766). The ability to improvise, and become good at it, seemed, at the time, to be an imperative if one was to survive each day's experience of working in an unpredictable environment with groups of lively children in a large comprehensive school on Merseyside. Retrospectively I can appreciate the influence of this early training on my work as a therapist and supervisor and on my development as a relational psychotherapist and supervisor. In her fascinating book about philosophical influences upon clinicians, Donna Orange (2010) discusses the influence of Martin Buber on humanistic thinking. The concept of 'confirmation', which formed a part of Buber's dialogic philosophy, is clarified in the following way: 'confirming [a] person *as he is* is only the first step'. For Buber confirmation of the client or patient involves the therapist taking in the patient's 'dynamic existence, in his specific potentiality', a process which has to involve the therapist *feeling* this potential (Buber, 1999, pp. 242–3, as cited by Orange, 2010, p. 27). I now understand my use of improvisation as an intuitive way to develop the potential inherent in the children, enabling them to find so much more within themselves than they thought might be possible, using play and the imagination to pretend and discover.

Although improvisation is defined by Chambers as a creative process, more negatively it is described as 'to do anything without proper materials or preparation' (p. 766). Perhaps there is an argument then to suggest that improvisation is most successful when the source of creativity is based on a wealth of experience. Nevertheless, when training to be a psychotherapist, I was taught that spontaneity was a contaminated idea, leading, as it easily could, to flippancy, and worse, revealing hidden sadistic instincts that would be harmful to a client or patient. It was of course both appropriate and containing for trainee therapists to be wary of our intuitive impulses. We were taught to rely on the facts of the situation, test any intuitive hypothesis with those facts, and to make a clinical diagnostic case for any interventions made. This rigorous type of training set the scene for a containing, ethical and professional practice, providing a secure environment to work with suffering people. The training provided a model of ongoing personal research, in which the clinician learned how to measure her use of interventions so she could be as effective a psychotherapist as it was possible to be: an ethical and professional goal worthy of all psychotherapists ambitious for the well-being of their clients or patients. Yet a crucial understanding about the nature of how people change was missing from this training, a fact I discovered by accident a few years after I had begun my private practice in the mid-1980s, prior to qualifying.

A vignette

I recall my work with a man who was possibly on the autistic spectrum, a condition I was unfamiliar with at the time. He spoke through the medium of his fascination and love for the composer Bartók, speaking in detail about Bartók's use of tonality, which apparently did not follow traditional lines of musicality. His detailed description of the numerical aspects of the music often sounded like arithmetic or algebra to my ears. With the benefit of hindsight and experience I can now see that he was trying to tell me something in code about his difficulty with emotional connecting. Impervious to this understanding at the time I tried to decipher what he was saying through the medium of my fascination with the theoretical perspectives of transactional analysis and person-centred psychotherapy. My response to my client's communication was to jump up quite frequently to a whiteboard (it was thought appropriate and helpful to have a whiteboard in one's TA consulting room) and draw circles and triangles on the board, referring to ego states (Berne, 1961) and the drama triangle (Karpman, 1968), trying, as I imagined, to respond empathically to what my client was telling me by converting it into circles and triangles. We must have looked a rather odd couple: him with his algebra and arithmetic and me with my geometry. To an onlooker it would have seemed as though we were speaking in 'tongues'! Nonetheless something important was happening under the surface as he continued his therapy, but I had no consciousness then of what that might have been.

About three months into the treatment, on the night before his session, my small son was ill and I spent a sleepless and anxious night tending to him. I cannot recall what the illness was but I was very uneasy and all the more so because any child's illness made me fearful and excessively anxious of pending loss, with its unconscious echo of my time spent in hospital as an infant, not that I thought about that at the time. Instead of cancelling the session, I stoically carried on. However I was not in my 'fascinated with my theory' mode. Instead I was feeling vulnerable, and in the type of space between sleep and wakefulness that John Keats (1899) described as 'negative capability', when a poet is at his most creative. In this vulnerable state I was more reliant on my intuitive sense, and although I cannot recall what exactly I said, it seemed, from what he later told me, that it was the quality of my listening, infused by the uncertainty that sleeplessness can bring, and an attuned sensibility towards the sickness in myself and others, which most affected him. I was most conscious however of a feeling of discomfort that I was not doing my job properly and hoping my client did not notice. I was surprised therefore when, at the end of the session, my client stood up, picked up his briefcase, turned to face me and, after a pause, when it seemed that he might be deciding whether to comment or not, and in which I dreaded to hear him say he was leaving therapy, he thanked me for the session, telling me it was the best one so far. I could see the feeling in his eyes, and something about the vulnerability of his body was captured by the way his pinstriped suit seemed to wrap itself around him, reminding me of how an infant is protected in a shawl, leaving me feeling a deep sense of sadness as he left.

Feelings had finally got through to me – feelings he had been trying to convey in his obsession with Bartók's unconventional use of tonality. As I sat with my reflections, I noticed another emotion that was at odds with my sense that I had not done a very good job, it was a sense of my worth and value in those moments of meeting between us: my value as a human being. Something had happened that I had no theory for then, something intriguing and encouraging, leading me to think that maybe it was possible to be a good clinician whilst I strayed outside the strait jacket of concrete facts. Linking this to my work with children as a drama teacher I began to see how psychotherapy was potentially as intimately connected with artistic expression as it was with science (particularly medical science). My vulnerability had seemed to have the effect of a healing quality on the therapeutic relationship, my willingness to let go of 'facts', go with the 'flow' and improvise the session encouraged a connection at a feeling level. In Buber's words I was more open to the 'I-thou' of relatedness, no longer coming from the superior position of the one who knows, but from one who listens, is open to connection, is able to feel the potential for mutuality. He was no longer an 'it' to me, no longer an object I had to do something with. From these experiences I learned that there was a role for improvisation, intuition, playfulness and imagination within the therapeutic process. Thus it was that the use of improvisation and its close partner intuition influenced my attitude towards my clinical work and the development of relational supervision.

Emotional and psychological honesty in relatedness and Irwin Yalom

How hard it can be for us psychotherapists to own our darker thoughts and feelings that emerge in the therapeutic work. For this reason I found it exciting and liberating to read Yalom's bold style of writing in which he expresses his deepest and darkest feelings. He never attempts to hide behind the label of counter transference, but unequivocally and honestly owns the feelings as his own. For example, in 'Fat Lady', a case study from his book entitled *Love's Executioner* (Yalom, 1989) he gives an unashamed account of his excoriating counter-transference towards his fat patient. The combination of his honesty about his feelings and his ability to reflect on them means he can use the full sense of his self in the therapeutic relationship. It is this principle of *emotional integrity* that is central to and underlies the relational approach. In 'Fat Lady' it finally emerges that Yalom's earliest counter-transference of loathing his patient is a projective identification reflecting the extent of the client's self-hatred, which eventually she is enabled to articulate. Of central importance is Yalom's *quality* of listening, influenced by his honest reflections, which enables the patient to articulate her experience.

In the humanistic tradition there has been a tendency for the therapist to openly reveal feelings in the belief that being 'authentic' with the client in this way will be helpful, but this way of thinking does not take into account the unconscious dimension of the communication. Such emotional expressions are often experienced as overwhelming and bewildering. For example a therapist said to her client, 'I am feeling angry right now, listening to what you are saying'. The client felt perturbed and anxious, wondering how and why she had had this effect on her therapist. The therapist had no consciousness that her feelings needed to be contained, and the meaning of them examined before self-disclosure (Little, 2011). Of course sometimes feelings emerge so strongly it is difficult to not react because we 'are about as effective at stopping an emotion as we are at preventing a sneeze' (Damasio, 1999, p. 49). Nevertheless it is important to keep a part of our mind detached enough to employ an intellectual curiosity to reflect on possible meanings that will provide a gateway into the unconscious of our client because such feelings 'are poised at the very threshold that separates being from knowing and thus have a privileged connection to consciousness' (ibid.). The therapeutic skill involves us in allowing the emotion, acknowledging it but not necessarily expressing it. Through the process of projective identification the client was trying to tell Yalom what it was like to be her. She needed him to understand how negatively she felt about herself. I became curious about how it would be possible to connect with this bi-directionality (or projective identification) of the relational unconscious between therapist and client (a process that generates the deepest intimacy possible between two people), into the *experience* of supervision rather than only using the concept to define a person and situation.

Counter-transference and the interpersonal

Counter-transference is well documented (Freud, 1912; Heiman, 1940; Winnicott, 1949; Little, 1951; Racker, 1968). From a humanistic perspective Hargaden and Sills (2002), drawing on this literature and developing the inherent interpersonal potential of the transferential relationship, propose a relational perspective of counter-transference. They describe the dynamic and distinctive nature of transference and counter-transference, calling them 'domains', borrowing from Stern's idea of domains of self (1985). In particular they bring attention to the reciprocal nature of projective identification as a bi-directional process. Through a collection of case studies they describe how the therapist has to allow herself to be emotionally impacted, to use her 'self', to catch the feelings: 'it is the responsibility of the psychotherapist to acknowledge, recognise, and hear the drum beat of her own inarticulate heart longings, in the service of understanding the communication from her patient' (Hargaden and Sills, 2002, p. 69). The case studies show how the bi-directionality of the relational unconscious in action, how the

dynamics of transference and counter-transference involve two sets of unconscious processes interacting with each other in multiple levels of relatedness
which require examination. In this way of thinking about and working with
counter-transference experience, the internal world of the therapist's emotional life is implicated and relevant.

Ruptures in the therapeutic relationship

Throughout this book you will find definitions and clinical examples in supervision of the necessity for ruptures and enactments as a way of accessing dissociated material. Because of the dissociative nature of trauma (see below for
a fuller discussion of the meaning of trauma), ruptures are now understood to
be the way through which trauma is accessed. It has become clearer that for
this reason, it is vital for the therapist to allow for mistakes in the therapy, to
allow for cracks in the edifice of her theoretical understanding and to trust her
intuitive mind, so that the light can get in, so the trauma can be revealed and
metabolised, for new language to emerge to make meaning, in the reflective
containing presence of the therapist. To bring this idea more fully alive I demonstrate an example from my clinical practice with a particular focus on the
significance of language as a code through which the unconscious is revealed.

A vignette – la participation mystique (Lévi-Strauss, 1967)

At the end of a session with my client, whom I shall call Maria, I stood up
to open the door. Maria stayed on the couch organising the cushions, which
prompted me to call out that she didn't need to tidy the cushions as though she
hadn't been there. We are taught that it is preferable to avoid making an intervention outside the therapy 'hour', and certainly not to say anything intense
and pregnant with meaning at the end of the session. However the unconscious mind knows nothing of such professional etiquette or rules. Maria must
have tidied the cushions many times and I had not noticed, so why, on this day,
did I pause and make such an observation? I later came to understand that in
choosing these anodyne-sounding words, I had unwittingly played my part in
a rupture in the therapy, that I had inadvertently become involved in 'la participation mystique' (ibid.): 'You don't need to make it seem as though you
were never here.'

When we next met I learned that Maria had been extremely distressed in
the intervening weeks (there had been a break). She asked me angrily if I had
realised what an impact my words had on her? I had not. I was astonished but

also curious and relieved that we were both involved in an intense emotional engagement rather than the more usual cognitive interactions. She repeated my words, 'You don't need to make it seem as though you were never here,' saying how it had seemed to her that I was both impatient and directive, making her feel that she had been caught out doing something wrong but more than that, she had been shocked into a recognition that she often felt as though she should be invisible. As we reflected together on the process between us over the following months Maria gradually began to connect with intense feelings of terror and loss associated, we began to understand, with her ancestors' catastrophic experiences in Stalinist Russia, their exile, the terror and unbearable losses of home and their community as they made their desolate journey to a strange and alien land. What had previously been an inability to forge an emotional connection with time past was now possible through the feelings surfacing between us. She said, 'I came back to tell you that the key fitted and then show you what it was I found inside.' For Maria my words had been a code that provided a type of key. We had gone beyond the surface of things to reach the depths, from the conscious known to the unknown (Bachelard, 1958/1994). The language I had unwittingly used became the key to finding the emotional bridge between past and present, resuscitating dead selves, allowing for the recovery of self-worth and self-agency. We began to understand why Maria had consistently relied on cognition, defending herself so resolutely with an impressive array of geographical and historical facts. Because she had no tangible loss to mourn there was a disconnect between her internal and external life which manifested itself in a feeling of an emotionally unbridgeable space between herself and others. As we talked about Maria's sense of the impenetrability of her mother as though she was made of stone, I observed that the trauma had seemingly passed through her mother's milk into Maria, a metaphor she instinctively felt fitted.

Learning from ruptures and enactments

From the above example of an enactment that caused a rupture in the therapeutic relationship we can learn: that dissociation cannot be known consciously until a rupture in the therapeutic relationship exposes the client to previously unfelt experience; that we are reliant on the bi-directionality of the relational unconscious to reveal the relational cracks through which the light of the unconscious can get in; that this process depends on the therapist's trust in her intuitive self; and that our choice of language often provides the key or code to the unconscious, bringing to mind Lacan's conviction that the unconscious is structured like a language. These types of experiences in my clinical practice made me wonder how to think about supervision groups in such a way that we could discover the hidden narratives in the clinical material presented. In Chapters 3 to 8 the authors variously and skillfully demonstrate how the use of group process, the intersubjective experience in the group, not only brought deeper meaning to the clinical work, but the very act of sharing minds in such a deep way transformed them as therapists, and brought new meaning to their work.

My personal analysis and the unconscious

By the unconscious I am referring to that part of our psyche that is unknown to our conscious mind and can be a force for both creative and pathological enactments. The most profound influence upon me has been my personal psychological journey into the unconscious. My analyst often referred to the old French alchemical maxim which says that to find self we need to cut off our heads with a clean knife, leave it behind a tree and go deep into the forest. He repeated it many times as I hovered nervously on the outskirts of that metaphorical forest (the unconscious). I did cling onto the fact that I could, and indeed must, collect my head on the way back out of the forest. Moving from the more 'rational' understanding of linear ways of thinking promoted in classical transactional analysis towards this more circular way of understanding clinical material, drawing on the ideas of alchemical change involving the transformation of the negre (dark material) into gold (the psychological self), completely altered the way I understood the psyche, not only from a cognitive point of view but from my experience. I had previously been in group therapy in which I made some fundamentally important changes. I had wanted to see the therapist for individual work because of a sense of emptiness and an unspoken distress for which I could not find the words. The visit, alas, was a failure. Retrospectively I can see that the therapist was in the same condition as myself, had not penetrated the deeper layers within herself, and so could not help me.

At the beginning of my Jungian analysis I had a series of intense dreams, one of which was me sailing in a rowing boat to the other side of the world, a symbolic journey that took me into the universe of the soul. Concurrently with this journey in my own analysis I was teaching trainee psychotherapists and beginning to develop relational theoretical perspectives, looking for ideas and language in which to structure my experience in my clinical practice. Working with Beatrice, for example, (the client who prompted me to develop relational theory and whose journey is recounted in Hargaden and Sills, 2002), had been quite functional, but as I changed in Jungian analysis, sensing the difference in me, she intuitively and increasingly pushed the therapy into a deeper sphere. How can we understand this theoretically? It became obvious that relational work is predicated on the use of 'self' and finding 'self' or maybe 'selves'; that to find the self of the client we needed to look into ourselves. Rather ambitiously I decided to transfer these ideas about the unconscious into the creation of my relational approach to supervision. In some ways I was back in the drama hall with my students, drawing on my and their ability to improvise.

Setting up a relational supervision group

Although I was used to running small supervision groups I began to think about the potential in using larger group processes. What type of conditions and environment would be helpful in setting up a larger relational supervision group? Since one of the therapist's tasks is to use her 'self' by reflecting imaginatively on the emotional messages we are receiving from both 'self' and 'other', the question arises about how we get into these deeper layers of the therapist's 'self' in supervision. One source of inspiration came from my work with therapy groups, which I had begun in the early 1990s.

The intra-psychic and the interpersonal

Initially I had drawn on methods based on humanistic beliefs that the expression of feelings was a fundamental right, that catharsis was healing in itself, with the major focus being on the interpersonal. I think it fair to describe the modus operandi of the time as follows: cushions were often banged, emotions expressed forcefully and thinking employed to make 'sense' of it all. Catharsis was thought to be the main vehicle for change but it turned out that fundamentally nothing much altered.

In Jungian analysis the focus of interest became more reflective and connected with the intra-psychic internal world, unearthing deeper feelings rather than the surface emotionality I had previously expressed. The changes in me were mirrored in my practice. One concrete example of this was that members of the therapy groups I lead spontaneously stopped beating cushions, and other assorted paraphernalia of cathartic psychotherapy disappeared, mostly, and oddly, without any comment by members of the therapy group or indeed me – an example, perhaps, of unconscious relatedness. Instead, a reflective process emerged. Although feelings were expressed, they were somehow less emotionally driven, as though coming from deeper parts of the psyche. I noticed how the power of the group was increasingly authoritative and potent as they explored their subjective experiences, clashed with each other, recognised their different realities, metabolised, reflected on and became able to expand on multiple possibilities in their search for meaning.

The influence of Jungian analysis on my work was profound and far reaching, affecting me both consciously and unconsciously, and manifested itself in my work with therapy groups. The type of psychological space I offered enabled members to develop an intuitive bond from which they derived strength, satisfaction and increasing self-identity. This experience impressed on me the power inherent in a collective meeting of minds. How could this be translated into the supervision setting in an ethical way that did not involve doing therapy in this way?

Group theories

Over the years I have been privileged to participate in, and lead, many different groups in teaching, therapy and supervisory settings. I have integrated group theories for example those of Bion (1967), Berne (1966/1994), Rogers (1970) and Nitzun (1996), but have found it unsatisfactory to stay within one model. Instead, when developing relational theory I have learned how to rely on my 'intuitive self' to work as a group leader. Naturally this 'intuitive self' is informed by group theories (though not in such a way that it makes them independent of each other) and the extent of the leader's psychological resilience and ownership of her vulnerability. Group members intuitively sense the leader's psychological state, and it is this which shapes the group culture. The extent to which she has engaged with her own early traumas, how she understands the potential for unconscious re-enactment of her painful experiences and her narcissistic needs to avoid conflict and to be seen as 'good' are communicated to the group at an unconscious level. This largely unconscious process shapes the type of space that allows for enactments, disturbance and a group sense that there is no feeling that cannot be felt and reflected upon (Hargaden, 2014a). Alongside this fundamental principle of the therapist's psychological condition, my main focus when running a group is based on Berne's emphasis upon the creation of clear, firm boundaries, making the space a securely contained place in which feelings can be expressed and meaning emerge (1966/1994).

The use of language

Language is central to our work. It opens up other possibilities, extends our range of reflective capacity and deepens clinical consciousness. I initially introduced the language of relational psychoanalysis into the group by making links with existing humanistic concepts such as mutuality and reciprocity.

Within this relational context it became more possible to play with ideas, associate with literature, poetry, lyrics, politics and life events, all of which informed the dialectical processes of reflection, providing metaphors for the human experience. These ideas not only opened up a way of thinking that broadened our understanding, but also increased our psychological vocabulary. Our extended use of language increasingly provided a creative space in which to learn and grow without judgement. Gradually members became interested in relational theory and began to study writers who appealed to them. I suggested we begin each meeting with a study session in which a member presented an author or new perspective they had become interested in. Alongside this I encouraged open debate and discussion, having set up an online discussion group on relational theory.

The co-created environment is thus not an empathic or mirroring one alone (though that can of course be important) but one that nourishes through the dialect and paradox of difference. This experience is captured by a participant of one of the relational supervision groups in the early days.

> One of the things I learnt in the group was that it was okay to think and feel for myself and be congruent with my own experience, even when this did not accord with others and might have impact on others, sometimes negatively. I learned too about how to hold my reality alongside other realities in a way, which did not cancel out anyone else's experience and enriched the overall experience.
>
> (Hunt, IARTA booklet, pp. 57–8)

Through this way of sharing our minds, diverse thoughts which may be confronting, challenging or provocative paved the way for the development of many different 'third' minds. (See below for a definition and discussion of the meaning of 'the third'.)

The Balint Chair

I borrowed from the idea of the Balint Chair to set up the structure of the group. The Balint Chair is named after the psychoanalyst Michael Balint (1957), who, together with his wife Enid, began a series of groups to support GPs gaining a more psychological understanding of the issues their patients presented. They used a method by which the presenter brought a case. Everyone in the group listened respectfully, making observations based on the tone, mood and style of the delivery. When adapting this method I suggested a member of the group present a case, giving us basic facts, revealing their feelings and experiences, and then staying silent as we discussed the case. I adapted the Balint Chair by inviting a personal and introspective process, asking members to focus on any feelings whatsoever that emerged, and to allow themselves to randomly associate, and to notice any sensations in their bodies. I wanted to free minds from theoretical formulations, to find a gateway into the unconscious.

This proved quite difficult. It involved a discipline of the mind to refocus on self in this way rather than relying on cognition. It is of course very difficult for a group of psychotherapists who are knowledgeable and interested in theoretical formulations to shift from thinking and hypothesising, and instead to allow a space for the emergence of the imagination: to leave certainty behind and delve into the terrain of the underworld. I say more about this process and examine the challenges for me in Chapter 9.

Fives phases of the relational approach to supervision

It became clear that everyone thought they were relational but with quite diverse ideas about what they meant. For instance while some understood the term 'relational' to be synonymous with interpersonal relatedness, others thought relational meant always being in an empathic mode, and some had ideas about the significance of the unconscious.

I made clear that the underlying principle for this way of working was based on the concept that the client's unconscious would be found in the therapist's unconscious (Bollas, 1987). This perspective is linked to an understanding of the unconscious nature of trauma. Trauma is defined by experience that has been so overwhelming it has not been metabolised, but exists in dissociated parts of the psyche, and is inaccessible through cognitive means, yet has injurious hidden influences on us. We had therefore to approach the whole project by learning to be comfortable with symbols, representations and uncertainty of meaning: to avoid, where possible, concrete understanding and uniformity of meaning. As a result it was important to create a clinically flexible supervisory structure whilst at the same time having a coherent focus. I suggested a group structure with five phases: i. clinical presentation; ii. group process in response to the presentation; iii. group reflection on the group process; iv. theoretical perspectives; and v. dialogue with the presenter.

i. Clinical presentation

The presenter is invited to speak about their client or patient. This involves giving us basic information about the person, such as age, race, sexuality, amount of time in therapy and other known facts, such as a brief reprise about their history and present-day circumstances and what the client or patient wants from their therapy. The presenter then describes his feelings in response to the client. Often, at this stage, the therapist will say warm and kind things about the client, and strive to be as understanding as they can. At this point I encourage the therapist to dig deeper and reveal the feelings he notices within him if he concentrates on his internal world. Questions are kept to a minimum as the presenter speaks, and then he sits in a chair outside of the group where he can observe the process. He makes notes about his responses to the group and anything he finds particularly useful.

ii. Group process in response to the presentation

At this phase I encourage the group to share feelings, random thoughts and associations and to dialogue with each other, to express feelings and thoughts which do not necessarily make any sense. I want to enable an environment in which dialectical discussion can take place without anyone trying to ana- lyse it, a space in which the original narrative of the presentation can become disorganised: to allow for a kaleidoscopic process in which meanings can change, alter and transform into many possibilities. I encourage a creative, imaginative and playful process in which we may even do impromptu role plays with each other.

iii. Group reflection on the group process

This phase is a place in which we can make meaning through reflection when the group can draw on their theoretical knowledge, use of metaphor and any thoughts that come to mind to reflect on the dynamics we have been involved in. The containing idea here is a shared understanding of how our minds develop through the use of the reflective function (Fonagy *et al.*, 2004). As an integral part of this reflective process I encourage the use of 'thirds' as a way of containing the dialectics of an intense discussion.

The 'third'

The' third' refers to the creation of a triangular *symbolic* space which can emerge from a collision of polarities in which a third way is formed. Gerson (2009) suggested three categories of potential thirds: developmental, cul- tural and relational. The developmental third represents the metaphorical father, who interrupts the therapeutic dyad and is represented in the work of Britton as an Oedipal constellation when his patient feels abandoned by his silence and tells him to stop 'that fucking thinking' (1989, p. 88).

The cultural third is one that envelops and shapes the interactions of the dyad as described earlier in my experience with the Irish client. In the initial stages we both shared a cultural third, which was Irishness, in the time of 'the Troubles', which was a symbol of a troubled history of colonisation and famine. This shared cultural third shaped the discourse between us. In an uncanny re-enactment of history, the patriarchal culture of the hospital, represented by the supervisor, dismissed our shared culture as irrelevant (just as Irish laws and Irish ways had once been dismissed by their colonisers); the supervisor, informed by the culture of patriarchy, killed our relationship, just as once the famine had wiped out millions of Irish people, thus recreating another third, described by Gerson (2009), when examining the psychological effects of the Holocaust as the 'dead third'. For further understanding of 'the developmental third', read the work of Chasseguet-Smirgel (1974) and Gabbard (1992).

The relational third is most frequently associated with an intersubjective perspective, as developed in the work of Ogden (1994) and Benjamin (2004). It refers to an innate sense of self with other that we bring to every meeting; it is the process by which we share experience with each other both consciously and unconsciously. There are overlaps between these categories of thirds, such as the developmental intersubjective third, the cultural intersubjective third and so on. The clinical benefits of thinking about 'thirds' are many, one of which is to enable the leader and members of the group to find their way out of binary processes using the 'third' as a symbol. Incorporating these ideas into the therapeutic and supervisory relationship introduces the possibility for more nuanced and discriminating forms of relating to both self and others.

The group situation offers an ideal opportunity for the evolution of thirds as metaphorical material through which discourse can take place. For instance each person in the group offers a 'third' eye, and the group itself becomes a 'third' mind. In addition, the presenter, sitting outside the group in the Balint method, offers another 'third' mind. In this phase, use of the third enables the group to situate thoughts and feelings that feel too dangerous into a place where it is possible to reflect on the binaries, potential meanings, rather than only be in the process of it. In such an environment there is no thought that cannot be reflected on, nor any feeling too dangerous to dwell on.

iv. Theoretical perspectives

This phase provides the opportunity for the group to play with theoretical formulations which emerge naturally through the relational process. It is often influenced by a study period of an hour, which is held at the beginning of each meeting, before any presentations, and in which we study themes for the year, with examples such as trauma, group work, the dead mother syndrome, hysteria and an exploration of the underlying philosophies that underpin psychotherapy. Each member makes a presentation, often drawing on a wide variety of writers, particularly from the relational psychoanalytic school. This provides a shared theoretical context that influences the group's reflections on the clinical material presented later.

v. Dialogue with the presenter

Now it is the presenter's turn to make his observations about the group process – how he has observed us. He is invited to describe his feelings and thoughts, which can prompt further dialogue in which new meanings may emerge as the presenter's mind and the client' s mind come more into focus.

In the following six chapters the relational approach is demonstrated through the subjective experience of former and current participants of a group. Each contributor reflects their own passions and intellectual development, consequently presenting their unique theoretical contribution to our understanding of relational theory in the context of relational supervision.

Chapter 2

The dialectical interplay between modes of relatedness in relational supervision

Brian Fenton

It is proposed by Benjamin that 'the relational perspective may be best characterised as an enquiry into questions of common concern that come to the fore as a result of the adoption of a two person model' (Mitchell and Aron, 1999, p. *xviii*). This situating of a two-person psychology and by implication a third subjectivity, namely intersubjectivity, as the central feature of relational psychotherapy, is a powerful notion. From this it follows that two-person models are also central to relational supervision. While it can be said that we organise our minds both intra-psychically and interpersonally, it is the interpersonal, and in particular the psychological and emotional processes within intersubjectivity in here-and-now relatedness, which is leading practitioners to reconsider how to effectively use our minds as therapists and supervisors. However, our existential reality remains that of experiencing self as oscillating from self as separate to self as self-other. This chapter reflects on some questions that come to the fore when we include a two-person model into the supervisory process. From this I propose that an understanding of the dialectics of relatedness will further facilitate a relational stance. To demonstrate this I am using an example of personal experience as a supervisee in group supervision where the group acts as a third mind. I then show the interconnectedness of psychotherapy and supervision and the use of different modes of relatedness in the formation of an empathic mind.

Two-person perspectives

The term 'two-person' has different meanings: ontological – a philosophical perspective on self-development; and epistemological – a mode of interaction, at times agreed as in therapeutic contracts. In this chapter my reflections largely sidestep concerns of ontology to focus on epistemology and the function of relatedness as these pertain to relational supervision. I take the position that it is where we are bringing our mind at any given moment that matters in the work, and that this will have functional implications for self-development. With this emphasis on epistemology we can proceed to consider the inclusion of two-person approaches into psychotherapy and supervisory practice.

A two-person model is one that recognises a third subjectivity, part me part you, and neither one nor other; where self and other together are more than the sum of their parts. Within this co-created space one can directly access the other's emotional experience (Hargaden and Fenton, 2005). This third subjectivity highlights the notion of a shared subjectivity and is for me the basis of what is termed two-person relatedness and co-creation (Summers and Tudor, 2000). While relationships exist within a matrix of experiences between self and other, this two-person relatedness is a driving force in how we transform our sense of self and other.

That intersubjectivity is a third subjectivity has particular relevance in that intersubjectivity has the effect of loosening boundaries between self and other (Aron, 2013), signifying a shift away from clear notions of one or other, this or that, including at times supervision or psychotherapy. One might consider social constructionism (Vygotsky, 1962) and variants of object relating within, including mimicry and identifications, projective identifications (Sandler, 1993) and non-verbal ulterior relatedness, as all conducted through the conduit of intersubjectivity. Holding an intersubjective framework requires a belief in a self that is born interpersonal and at some level always interconnected (Stern, 1985; Trevarthen, 1993; Winnicott, 1985). This notion of always being connected is inherent within a post-modernist situated self, where self and context are bound. A post-modern perspective of relativity also includes within it the notion of bi-directional effect and ambiguity as regards direction of effects and in doing so questions certainty itself.

Unconscious process group (the initial name for what became known as the relational supervision group)

On qualifying as a Certified Transactional Analyst I joined an 'unconscious process group' run by Helena Hargaden. Prior to this I had an experience post qualification of knowing I was perfectly adequate but not feeling it. I recall revealing this dilemma to a dear tutor and mentor, who responded by saying all they could see was a confident able practitioner. Whatever their intention this felt like a negation of my subjective experience. At the time I hadn't realised this comment revealed a core issue between relational transactional analysis and the more traditional classical perspectives within TA. The main area of difference was that from a relational perspective there was more of a focus on entering into our inner subjective worlds directly through intersubjectivity (including unconscious and non-verbal relatedness), whereas in traditional methods of TA there was more of an emphasis upon the external, linked to the cognitive-behavioural roots of TA, which typically engages with what is wanted and ignores that which is maybe needed, and unknown to the person.

My initial TA training, which was integrative, was enormously life changing, and I am glad of it. However the gap between what I felt I should feel like now that I was a trained therapist and what I actually felt like was unfortunately widened by the theoretical disparity between cognitive knowledge and subjective experience. This led to an increase in my psychological and emotional distress. Something of my core self was being missed.

In the relational supervision group the emphasis, when presenting a client, was on resisting moving too quickly into cognitive knowing. There was a steering too on group members to focus on feelings they had in response to the presentations. At times the feelings expressed were hostile and primitive and the meanings that emerged from these were unpalatable. I recall being troubled by the insistence of the group on holding on to the notion of ambiguity, as opposed to my normal response of being quick to analyse, and by responses to my presentations, such as anger, which initially I took personally. In hindsight I now know this to be two-person relatedness in the group process, which allowed for potential split-off elements of the client or therapist to emerge from within group members' subjectivities, providing emotional material for reflection. I recognised my desire for sameness and associations related to conflict avoidance present in the group. It was also present in my clinical work. The ambiguity of the group process reminded me of a book where the ending is frustratingly uncertain. I learned that clarity, if it came, would come from group process as opposed to thinking about the original narrative expressed by the client and therapist. I came to understand that while cognitive understanding such as the traditional approach within TA to analyse script (influences upon the client) has a function in raising self-awareness, the process of self-development has another level, one that demands a more immediate experience between client and therapist and at times therapist and supervisor.

I learned experientially that feelings I was having in response to clients were potentially counter-transference and not necessarily just about me. These unconscious processes brought my mind to levels of relatedness where we are unaware of our interconnectedness. I began to understand that we are not as separate as we like to think we are, and that we are both separate and connected. Although we have conscious explicit knowings of being separate and simultaneously projective implicit knowings within intersubjective connectedness I also realised that the connectedness is not necessarily script (Berne, 1961) but existential reality. These understandings sparked a personal interest in two-person relatedness and its functions in self-development. This recognition re-stimulated my interest in my psychology degree. In particular I was influenced by the work of Trevarthen (1979) on primary and secondary intersubjectivity, which, in collaboration with Helena, resulted in our paper (Hargaden and Fenton, 2005), where we explored non-verbal transactions. From this I ventured further into dialectics and to our existential situation of being self and self-other.

Including two-person approaches in supervision

The inclusion of a two-person approach requires accommodation. This includes expanding on existing concepts in psychotherapy and, following on from this, supervision. To exemplify we can consider the example of empathy in relation to levels of relatedness and development of mind.

Vygotsky (1962) proposes that the capacity of the infant to develop an organising subjective perspective about self and others is dependent on the mother's empathic involvement in her infant. This situates experiencing empathy as central to developing reflective capacity as evidenced by Schore (2000). Vygotsky goes on to suggest that the mother draws the infant into her world of meanings. There is then both a need to be 'held in mind' accurately (Fonagy and Target, 1998), as in to be attuned with, and also, through the drawing of the infant into the mother's world of meanings, a need to provide a frame for the other to think with and push against. We need the mind of another from which to find our own mind, and we do this in different modes.

For example, one-person perspectives may view empathy as purely an imaginative activity. Rogers describes empathy as the 'therapist … experiencing an accurate empathic understanding of the client's awareness, of his own experience. To sense the client's world as if it were your own, but without ever losing the "as if" quality' (1990, p. 226). This insistence on 'without ever losing the "as if" quality' suggests that entering into the other's experience rests on our capacity for imagination, using elaborations from our own actual relational experiences. We remain in our own shoes.

However, a two-person perspective questions the position of never losing the 'as if' quality. Firstly, if we extend our understanding of phenomenological experience to include notions of being taken beyond ourselves and into self–other phenomenological experience such as with counter-tranference and projective identification, and view these to varying degree, as forms of co-construction (a third subjectivity), we can see then that self can initially be found in the other through relatedness. In this instance through bringing potential emotional narrative to projective identifications, we can use our self as therapists from our world of meanings, to support clients to find their world of meanings. An eye towards two-person engagement then takes us beyond our conscious imaginations, perhaps through mirror neurons (Allen, 2011), into feeling states that reside in the intersubjective third space and into the shoes of the other. We are in effect using here-and-now experience to inform our sense of other, and this includes non-verbal and unconscious processes. From the revealing of self–other intersubjective experiences we at times have to work to untangle whose mind is whose (Maroda, 2004). This untangling, such as through these processes being revealed in supervision, furthers empathic relatedness in its cognitive sense, through enhancing self–other differentiation at a conscious level of relatedness.

Importantly though, empathising with another's position does not necessarily mean we agree with it, nor should therapists who intend to use themselves in the process feel that they must. The emerging understandings from intersubjective relatedness might reveal disagreement. From the holding of one's own position this can encourage separateness, and a modelling that alignment is not necessary for relationship to proceed. The objective is more then to achieve a fuller understanding of the other's position, which at times results in an understanding where we can lose classical empathic qualities such as warmth, through for example the recognition of our value systems being incompatible. Differences at these points bring with them potential for co-creating resilience, a tolerating of authenticity, and contribute towards a repair distinct from agreement. Underlying these processes are subtle attitudes influenced through one's own psychological defences, which in the therapist's case can emerge in the supervision process.

Incorporating a two-person approach into the dialectics of existence

Arguably by accepting that we are existentially dialectical leads to a recognition of competing motivations such as homeostasis – actualisation. We also have different levels of relatedness such as unconscious and conscious which may or may not be in tension, and we experience self as both separate and as together. That we are dialectical must have some bearing in the emergence of, and the management of, the contradictions of being, and ultimately the framing of a theory of mind itself.

The dialectical process utilised by philosophy is one where there is a hypothesis as well as its contradiction, the antithesis, resulting in an emerging third position: the synthesis of these two. Synthesising includes the notion of a mutual and reciprocal interaction of both situations (Engels, 1888, p.217). This process has been worked and reworked (Hegel, 1874; Marx, 1873; Hoffman, 1998) and seems to me to remain of value to relational perspectives which are inherently interested in our fuller existential dilemmas. The vitalising energy within the synthesising process leads to the destruction of the old and the creation of something new, both in philosophy and in self itself. This process is frequently seen in our cultural models, such as conflict models (Freud, 1940; Berne, 1964; Goulding and Goulding, 1978; Mellor, 1980), and perhaps in the notion of humanism itself being the third wave of psychology. While stepping out of dialectics frees thought through creating reflective third positions, the process of dialectics itself remains developmental.

Understanding unconscious process group

Being exposed to so many ideas and perspectives on mind in the group resulted in my experiencing the dialectics of relatedness in action. In particular, considerations of who was who at levels of relatedness and knowing one's own mind co-existed. An attempt to hold these understandings triggered a lack of self-confidence within me which had survived my initial training therapy. This lack of confidence was related to difficulties I was experiencing in managing seeming contradictions in myself. Splits in the group triggered splits in me. While there was support on how to think about what was happening in group process from the group leader and the other participants, there was equal weight given to the freedom to finding our own minds.

It seems that relational perspectives could expand on the method of philosophical enquiry described above and focus on interpersonal dialectics. Through this expansion we can reconsider the meaning of dialectics and their relationship to self-development. While dialectics, as a philosophical activity, may function to bring polarities together and bridge disciplines (Hoffman, 1998), the process need not be reduced to ironing out difference by achieving sameness. For example where we have two opposing forces the new third position, the synthesis of the two, may not be one of agreement. For instance there may be agreement to disagree, and still contribute to a new universal holding theory, as is the case in post-modernism, which brokers a temporary peace between innate self and contextual pluralities by adopting a *both/and* approach (Batts, 1983).

When applying dialectics in this form to human relatedness, where no two people can ever be the same, we can then focus not on achieving sameness or necessarily ironing out difference, but on arriving at some new mind through the struggle. This position, where sameness is impossible, points us to the significance of framing therapy as an art form, where on the canvas so to speak we can mix elements of humanity that do not sit well within a scientific frame. Yet these elements fit within our real world experience of being. This position is furthered by Fonagy (1999), who reminds us that the mechanisms of each therapy will be individualised according to patient and therapist, meaning *there is no one mode of therapeutic action*. This brings an understanding of why we have different stances with each client, which is in itself meaningful in terms of clinical presentation.

Our dialectic situation then raises the need to extend phenomenological experience to include our phenomenological difference when with different people, which also questions the idea of self as a constant. Yet experientially we feel continuous over time and context. It seems to me that there is something of value in both positions, and that as we exist as self and as self-other, both need to be accounted for.

Unconscious process group (continued)

My anxieties in the group continued to unfold, triggering a process of self-object relatedness in supervision. With hindsight this process emerged through my need for protection from what I felt at times to be attacks through others expressing different minds. These experiences of feeling attacked were often related to my own process of seeking sameness and a form of single-mindedness associated to primitive separation anxiety. While a potential source of disturbance for the supervisor to manage and contain, this self-object process acted as a motivating force for me, just as it can do in psychotherapy. Two-person relatedness was then emerging directly between my supervisor and me. While the focus of relational supervision is on a positive outcome for the client, how this is achieved differs from traditional methods of supervision in that client outcome is seen to be improved by encouraging the therapist at times to develop their own mind through the supervisory relationship. In responding to this situation Frawley-O'Dea and Sarnet (2001) suggest that a rigid demarcation between teach and treat is not compatible with a relational approach, and that as long as the supervisee and supervisor are clear with each other as to the 'overarching goal of facilitation of the supervisee's growth as a clinician' (p. 140), then this guideline legitimises elements of supervisee self-development occurring in supervision. Whereas teach-treat from a one-person perspective has a clear boundary, when including the two-person process this boundary can be ambiguous. While unconscious processes occur within their own remit, we can presume the tasks of therapy and the tasks of supervision shape emerging identifications to a point, guiding the supervisor's responses to them.

These types of relational learnings go beyond theory or method to include here-and-now identifications from how a supervisor responds and considers process in the group. Ultimately influencing the practitioner's internal supervisor (Casement, 1985), the identifications can range from feeling a sense of a supervisor's guiding interventions to a more introjective experience of finding oneself 'being' one of them in the practice room. Understanding this process of identification led me back to a two-person perspective through Vygotsky, who suggests that 'the very mechanism underlying higher mental functions is a copy from social interaction; all higher mental functions are internalized social relationships' (1988, p. 74). We can hypothesise from this also that concrete experience of being led to notice unconscious phenomena through the mind of a more able other (a therapist or supervisor) leads to the development of the ability in the practitioner to be more symbolic in thought and alert to metaphoric language.

While self-object relating need not necessarily signal a need for therapy, for me it did. The dilemmas I was faced with were related to being able to notice and own my aggression and shadow partly in relation to my anxiety, and to be able to determine whose mind belongs to who at levels of relatedness. I found that the associated anxieties impaired my ability to utilise the experience of the group, to the point where supervision as a harbour was being lost, at times experiencing it as more anxiety-raising than containing.

Knowing ourselves primarily as a benchmark from which we can recognise others is important in the endeavour to work with unconscious processes. It is also important in that enactment and potential rupture from this can be as much about us not knowing parts of ourselves as it is about clients not knowing elements of themselves. The defensive anxiety we experience regarding these unknown unacknowledged elements of our own selves can prevent recognition of the bi-directional effect of relatedness.

I realised that I needed to come to know my more primitive process and get to grips with different levels of relatedness. This led me to enter psychoanalysis, which was itself a challenge, as the experience was much less interpersonal than the forms I was used to. At times I felt the method lacking in mutuality and too one-person in orientation. That said, the frequency of twice-a-week sessions and the managing of what seemed at times like an intolerable space left for me by my analyst led to an intense engagement. My experiences of tolerating anxiety in the unconscious process group supported my management of this therapeutic experience. Through the reflection on subtle feelings and thoughts such as the meaning of when and why my analyst responded, or seemed to not respond, I was able to come to recognise and then understand my own mind. The outcome of this therapy was that I became more able to boundary the self-object concerns that had been appearing in supervision. Simultaneously the self-other concerns I had been experiencing in supervision and therapeutic practice became easier to identify, as did my need for sameness. I felt more able to be myself and to appreciate difference and gained the confidence to stay with ambiguity.

I learned from the group that meaning is negotiated, and that within the relational approach there are multiple positions to adopt functionally, such as holding the boundary and reflecting on a client's experience of the space, and also to consider when to openly share my mind, or reflect on the consequences of an unintentional slip. The mix of personal psychotherapy and group supervision brought me a holding of a different kind. I became able to notice my own difficulties in relationships, which brought clarity, as I became more sensitive to noticing the more subtle pushes and pulls of relatedness, first in myself and then in my clients.

In the group I experienced intersubjectivity in action not only between self and other but also as scattered or fragmented elements of experience, gathered by the group participants from their subjective experience in response to my client presentations. Being led to bring our minds to emerging feelings, reverie and associations in the search for unconscious process was particularly productive. Group members offering seemingly random thoughts and feelings that arrived in their minds supported access to the primitive processes of relatedness. At times, when these emerging feelings and thoughts led to dead ends, the act of reflecting itself served to fashion our minds to the task. From this I came to understand that these emerging insights are not necessarily to be put back to the client; more that they are collected in the therapist's mind as potential communications, primarily for understanding and consideration of how to proceed in any specific client work.

Different mindsets and their functional significance

While we see through our minds, our minds are governed by our contexts and our natures. The emphasis of social construction on our situated self has the effect of taking our eye off our nature and potential restrictions on fluidity. Governing forces of self, such as those termed love, spirit, temperament and innate protocols and mechanisms on how to be, are also important and highlighted in script (Berne, 1972), archetypes (Jung, 1990), grammar (Chomsky, 1965), morals (Hauser, 2006), splitting (Klein, 1959) and language games (Wittgenstein, in Stroll 2002). These forces are all mediated within relational matrices through intersubjectivity.

These governing forces and protocols can be demonstrated through Wittgenstein (1980), who viewed language as 'a form of human rule-governed activity, integrated into human transactions and social behaviour, context-dependent and purpose-relative' (p. 461). Commenting on this phenomenon, Heaton and Groves (1994) suggest language 'depends on many underlying non-linguistic features, above all on human nature' (p. 113). They go on to suggest that if the death of a friend had no human significance to us we would not be able to understand the language, gestures and rituals of mourning. This last point distinguishes between types of thought and points to different mindsets. By this I mean when reflecting with someone on thoughts and feelings related to attachment issues, these exchanges are distinct and contain ordained knowings and powerful motivations which highjack our minds and underlie emerging cognitions. For example abandonment process triggered in adult relatedness serves to offer us a sense of control and a way out of feeling the vulnerability of mourning. Wittgenstein, that genius of logic, then points us to other worlds within, where the logic is concerned with other matters, such as psychic survival and developmental concerns (Bowlby, 1958), which demand to be met interpersonally. While naming presenting issues may offer some holding in mind as to what is causing our distress (i.e. you are in mourning), the way forward will more likely require a relational working through of the mourning process. Intersubjectivity belongs to this relational world within a mindset distinct from cerebral cognition alone, and is principally concerned with managing self-other relatedness.

The idea of different mindsets was furthered for me within notions of one- and two-person psychologies. Gill (1994a, 1994b) describes one-person innate intra-psychic self-organising forces, where to borrow the Gouldings' (1978) term, the power can be said to be in the patient. Gill also describes two-person self-organising forces where we might consider the power to reside more between patient and therapist within the relationship. Gill includes the notion that these self-organising experiences occur simultaneously (Silverman, 1996). Reflecting further on the functions of different mindsets being implicated in self-development I turned to Stark (1998), who extends Gill to describe three modes of relatedness: one-, one-and-a-half, and two-person. Stark views these positions as types of psychological relationship affiliated with therapeutic method. One-person, as in the classical Freudian model; one-and-a-half-person, where there is a more interpersonal participation between therapist and client, and two-person, where there is an emphasis on the reciprocal, mutual relating process ranging from the implicit to open self-disclosure. These forms of relatedness in themselves demonstrate the complex nature of psychological and emotional development and for me pointed away from single-mindedness and towards the dialectics and existential contradictions of relatedness as all having a function in the development of mind. The therapist's task is to make mindful, flexible, therapeutic intervention as the 'required relationship' (Little, 2013) emerges, and to consider why we oscillate from mind to mind at any given time with any one client.

Vignette

My initial encounter with Peter was in weekly one-to-one therapy throughout his TA training. It wasn't the easiest of relationships: he, a diligent and competent student of classical transactional analysis; me, a fledgling relational therapist. There was throughout our work a sense of my not doing it right for him, which at times felt more concrete than symbolic. Peter had suffered complex trauma, abuse, neglect and abandonment. This was combined with his having moved continents as a teenager and his support networks being forcibly disrupted, leaving him quite lost in a strange land – just as he felt in this therapy.

Peter's disappointment in me manifested in such things as my not overly praising him and telling him how bright he was (he was in fact a very competent student, though plagued with not feeling good enough). While I was experienced as withholding, in response to this, his deeper feelings of inadequacy emerged for reflection. Our initial work together involved Peter's putting his experiences of us through his mind and finding his own edges through my adopting a one-person stance where we both focused on his mind. Peter curtailed and was deeply troubled by hostile fantasies towards me (in these he imagined throwing me round the room, smashing me against the wall). His more explicit longing was to be close to me, and these emerging implicit elements to punish and destroy me were in tension, resulting in agitation, further anxiety and a hostile dependency.

What Peter wasn't to know was that I was working to figure out my experience of him in supervision. In particular I was working through the inadequacies I felt in relation to him, and to understand more my desire to soothe him. My own inadequacies of 'not doing it right', my competitiveness as a man (in the face of his formidable force) and the remnants of a matching macho script process, where 'boys don't cry', were evoked. Combined with my developing understandings regards empathy and separate minds, learning to tolerate feeling 'bad' because of not feeling empathetic enough was consistently challenged in the unconscious process group. Here the right to have one's own mind in the process was seen as important, at very least in terms of providing opportunity for relational development.

Bringing my mind to my own process in supervision left me more able to know Peter as different from me, and while I could support him, he had his own battles to fight. As a result of this understanding, my own anxieties became more easily contained, in that I could situate them. This left me more confident in offering counter-transference feelings back into the mix for co-reflection, and to reflect on Peter's anxieties and expectations of me. From this repetitive ongoing process Peter's symptoms subsided. In particular his embodied dreams, where he would be having arguments while asleep, to the point that he would often wake his partner with fits of aggression, abated. It seems to me that he had developed more of a sense of 'I', and was more able to appropriately contain and regulate his own self.

That said, Peter remained anxious right to the end of his first bout of therapy. An unresolved theme of power and control remained, which manifested in the question of fees. At the time I was unable to get hold of it and tended to treat the process at a concrete level. I said to myself that he was a man who was struggling financially and trying to change his life (a theme I could relate to, and one that perhaps diminished my empathic response through self-other mix-up). To accommodate him, or perhaps with hindsight to avoid his aggression, I would periodically reduce my fee, and not pay adequate attention to the meaning of those 'forgotten' cheques. The issue was never about Peter not paying (he had integrity and always paid) – it was about *when* he paid. At the end of his last session, before leaving, Peter 'forgot' his fee. My heart sank as I felt something central was missed.

Peter returned a few years later, reporting that his aggression was escalating, and that he had even got into a physical fight. He wanted to come back to 'do his therapy'. Contextually he had cut loose from the authority of the therapy world, and had returned to body-building to cover his internal fragility. His familial dilemmas were more florid than ever, and he felt unable to separate from a dysfunctional family system. By now I understood his dilemmas more, and the impossibility of his situation regarding the power within those bonds. We began to understand he was on a journey, one that he could not take his family on, even though he loved them and could not leave them behind. While I hoped to be able to support him as he came to some new understanding regarding his situation, I knew his dilemmas were more than attachment beliefs keeping him bound; they were embedded in his real world of familial relatedness.

Peter's working-class roots clashed with the dominant one-person ideologies of the classical therapy world of his training, where aspiration is understood to come from within. This is problematic in that it brings with it an emphasis on notions of responsibility and choice, which can inadvertently compound self-recrimination. There is also from this perspective an attitude embedded within, of 'we can be anything we want to be if we just will it', stemming from unrealistic expectations of social mobility. A two-person perspective views aspirations as more contextually situated, which points us to the political and the recognition of the influence of wider social constraints, and more directly at an interpersonal level: the power the familial has on mind through intersubjective process (Kondo, 1990). Peter's therapy would include developing an understanding of the nature of contexts, and how some paths are more difficult to traverse. Being mindful regarding leaving him space to find his own mind, I also felt able to offer intuitive assumptions on potential dilemmas, holding his wider context in mind. From my own experience of these challenges I could draw Peter into my world of meanings (a more one-and-a-half-person approach, where provision is not in resonating with the need per se but in the provision of mindful consideration of a situation). This time round I felt more confident as a therapist and anticipated something unfinished would emerge between us. Although I felt ready I was caught by surprise as my authority was attacked.

We had been talking about unfairness within the asymmetry of our relationship and were, to my mind, getting somewhere. These sessions led us in different directions – at times into a process of talking about seemingly unrelated issues, such as when he arrived in England, frightened, bullied at school and in a bleak, depressing situation. The asymmetry in our relationship had in effect led through association to deeper issues of power and control, loss and mourning (language games related to abandonment and loss and processes that required a working through). At other times Peter would feel attacked by a seemingly insensitive intervention. After one session where he felt attacked by me, he was able to say he had had thoughts about me such as 'get your act together little man' (a potentially projected element of himself related to his body-building). Here we were again straight into my own anxieties about my inadequacy as a therapist and as a person, and the difficulties of managing a busy practice. Was I paying attention properly? I remained boundaried and co-reflected with him on how he was experiencing me. In doing so I provided Peter with some opportunity to express aggression and for him to hate me, as was denied to him in his developmental context through fear of reprisal.

Then during the next session Peter said that he had problems at home regarding money for building work, and needed to leave therapy for a month or two. On the surface it was apparently a reasonable request, but given our therapeutic history (and our contract to work through his difficulties), alarm bells rang. I was flabbergasted and angry with him, feeling put in an impossible situation. I felt quite unable to diminish my response, and empathy felt impossible. I interpreted the situation: while I could see just how anxious he was in telling me he needed to leave (i.e. fearing retribution), I felt unmovable and certain of my position. I told him I was unlikely to agree a break was the right thing, that I thought he needed to stay and work through this situation, and that I felt this was not solely about affordability. He felt trapped and experienced me as unreasonable. He also felt guilty and powerless as he did when asking his father for monies owed to him for work he had done (which his father only paid when he felt like it). Here we were adopting positions for each other in an all-or-nothing binary.

Dialectics and interpersonal enactments

Nowhere are interpersonal dialectics more evident than within emotional and psychological enactment (Bromberg, 1993). Here the working through directly between client and therapist and at times therapist and supervisor is emphasised. Enactments are not specific to a relational approach. However the inclusion of immediate two-person here-and-now relatedness makes encountering these processes more likely for relational practitioners. Also the inclusion of a two-person mindset extends possibilities in using the self in both considering and responding to these situations.

Vygotsky (1993) states that 'Development is precisely the struggle of opposites' (p. 283). Opposites bring to mind complementary opposites (Benjamin, 2002a) and power-laden dynamics including binaries. Binaries are by definition co-joined; one position cannot exist without the other. This situation recognises mutual reciprocal relating, and that element of our existence where we take up positions for each other within intersubjective relatedness, and in effect co-create the experience.

Opposites also lead me to reconsider Berne's *Games People Play* (1964) and the complementary psychological positions on the drama triangle (Karpman, 1968). The meaning of games in TA psychotherapy could be extended to include our participation with an innate agenda of furthering our subjectivity; an attempt to force our way to new mind, through the experiential working through of the polarities within binaries such as those termed relational units

(Little, 2004). These meetings of minds vary from those that feel caring and warm through to those that feel more like collisions.

One way to consider the interpersonal and intersubjective developmental process of dialectics is that when we retract that which was projected out into the third space (the relationship), our self is transformed through its having been fused with other (including the meaning we make of that within our own meta-reflecting selves). We might say the re-internalised identifications are a synthesis of self and other. These psychological binaries exist within intersubjectivity, and when noticed can be connection points and pathways, linking us dialectically both to the other and also through bi-directional effect to our own unknown selves. As unknowns these parts of self require influence from others for transformation to occur, which situates supervision at the heart of therapy itself.

Enactments generally occur when we are unable to notice self-other mix-ups, such as when we have blind spots (Ekstein, 1969), allowing their characteristic of unexpectedness to emerge. That change is at times mutual has effects on the therapist (and the supervisor), not least of which is the effect of mutual vulnerability (Aron, 2013). By this I mean that psychological and emotional change requires a relinquishing of boundary to take in other. At times, such as when working with unconscious process, this process of self-transformation involves a loss of control and the situation can feel unwanted or even forced upon us. When control is lost we are most vulnerable, as self-integrity is perceived to be threatened and psychological defences are activated. This vulnerability to anxious defence can, if managed well enough, lead to a situation where the self-other boundary is fluid. The latter is directly related to both the supervisor's and the therapist's attitude and sensitivity to what's occurring. Being mindful that being caught unawares can be akin to being seen in ways we do not want to be seen, which is a central component of shame (Shadbolt, 2009), reminds us of how challenging these processes can be. While we can work to build resilience in supervisees through experiencing situations in supervision and therapy, the 'being out of control' itself remains a vital element within the experience of enactment.

Vignette (continued)

Taking this process between myself and Peter to a different supervision group, I felt confident my colleagues would be equally indignant regarding my course of action. To my disappointment this was not the case. Mostly they empathised with Peter, leaving me feeling quite misunderstood. I felt dejected and alone with it. How could they not see that this was an enactment? The emerging process, where I felt trapped and not understood, revealed a deeper level of enactment between Peter and me. To change the dynamic I felt I was required to step off my own victim position and into his. Through this process of projective identification I felt more what it was like for him and realised I had been fixed in my victim position. I was then able to feel the extent of Peter's powerlessness through identifying with my own, and through tolerating this part of myself I felt stronger. From this position I felt less vulnerable to the tyranny of my own defences, from which I had wanted to fight back against what seemed like submission.

This process began as a split where it felt overwhelming, as if the whole group were against me. Through being able to dip in and out of this anxiety and regain my mind, I began to recognise defensive process in me from my earlier experiences in the unconscious group process, and was able to notice that the group wasn't so split at all, and that it was me in my own mind amplifying conflict and related anxieties. There were members of the group who empathised with my position. The supervisor played a role in holding contributions from others as material for consideration. From this group process third positions appeared, including that both Peter and I were in difficult positions. I felt my role was to manage the boundary of our contract, and he had to steel himself to challenge me and contain his anxious aggression. The combination of supervision and personal therapy facilitated my capacity to recognise my own process, and to then be able to tolerate the anxiety related to difference. From this I managed to maintain a level of reflectivity to work effectively, and my empathic capacity returned.

Even after the group had finished the rumblings in my mind continued as I worked to accommodate the process. On the way home, left to my own mind, I had a niggling anger at some of the interventions from my colleagues – they didn't know the full story, etc. I then realised they were offering me alternative viewpoints and possibilities, not directions, and that it was my own mind that was losing this quality. Regaining confidence from this more adult stance, I recognised that I did know Peter well and that we could discern our way forward. The knowledge gained in the unconscious process group supported and informed my being able to resist being overruled by what could seem a superior point of view, and to own my own subjective sense of the rightness of this unique situation. In particular I felt that holding the boundary had been the right thing to do. Even though I couldn't deny feeling trapped and misunderstood, the supervision process was illuminating data for the therapy; both things were true.

The next session, my mind changed, I was able to be more reflective. I felt able to own that while holding the boundary had felt right, I couldn't know for sure what was best for Peter. I was disappointed that while this seemed to me to be a missed opportunity I had to respect his autonomy. However Peter arrived with a different mind too. He had had a difficult week. His partner had wanted him to stay in therapy (as I did), alerting me to his wider social matrix of relatedness. Despite feeling resistant to these influences and wanting to have a mind of his own (Cornel and Bonds-White, 2001), Peter couldn't deny that he felt changed by my managing the boundary as I did. In response he seemed to have gained reflectivity and the ability to consider different levels of what had occurred. He had an 'inpouring' of experiences into his conscious mind, and more clarity about what boundaries he had never had placed as a child. He was more able to locate and to situate who he was angry with, and seemed more secure in his own mind. I realised through his struggle to find his own mind that I too had had a similar struggle for mind in supervision. Later, when reflecting on what had happened between us, I revealed some of my own process, such as the nagging uncertainty I felt about being certain, and my feeling trapped. What was evident for me was that I felt able to do this, as we had a more mature alliance and our relationship was changed.

Conclusion

This case example described the dynamic relationship between group supervisions, the client work, the personal development of the supervisee and how the latter can at times be situated in the supervisory process. It also demonstrated the differing relational mindsets active in the relatedness, such as in the oscillating between one-, one-and-a-half- and two-person modes. The synthesising of dialectical binaries between client and therapist, through the 'third' of intersubjectivity within group supervision process was demonstrated. Conscious and unconscious process and attachment mindsets intent on self-integrity and self-actualisation were also described, as were wider contextual factors.

The point of describing the dialectical process in this chapter is two-fold: to bring our minds to our contradictory natures in an effort to contain the complexity we as practitioners are faced with, both within ourselves and in the consulting room; and to consider what this self-organising force underpinning (and perhaps regulating) relationality might mean for relational supervision in how we consider adopting a two-person perspective.

Relational group supervision includes an experiential component which leads us in different ways to the relationship between supervisees and supervisor. As with psychotherapy itself, the situation exists in supervision of supporting supervisees to find their own mind through our minds, by drawing them into our world of meanings, while also leaving space for them to find their own mind. While the focus of relational supervision is to have a positive outcome for the client, how this is achieved differs in that client outcome is seen to be improved by supporting the therapist at times to develop their own mind through the supervisory relationship. With this in mind it seems to me that the tasks of development of the supervisee's discernment and that of overseeing client treatment are inextricably bound.

As with all relationships we can consider that there is an ongoing multiplicity of relational levels occurring simultaneously, and that these are a continuing theme of the supervisory relationship. In particular the attitude of practitioners towards asymmetry, and their ability to notice and tolerate intersubjective relatedness, contributes towards the formation and maintenance of empathic relatedness and ultimately the therapeutic alliance (Lambert and Ogles, 2004).

Apparently then the 'required relationship' pulls us to be flexible in approach, though at times only two-person engagement will suffice. Through being drawn into interpersonal dialectical processing, my clients and I adopt mutual binary positions within intersubjectivity, which if worked through between us, can be transforming for us both. In these situations I often need to be supported back on track in supervision, where my fuller mind is returned, and at times developed. As the Benjamin quote above forewarns, the adoption of a two-person perspective presents us with questions. For me this includes how to include existing concepts. Empathy has been shown to be constructed through combining modes of relatedness across contexts. While therapeutic empathy can lead to repair, empathic relatedness can also include robust disagreement and repair of a different sort.

A pressing issue for therapists in the consulting room is the freedom to practice based on the recognition that it is more the logic of our attachment mindsets, as opposed to what constitutes objective reality, that matters most in the activities of psychotherapy and supervision. The ambiguity brought by two-person modes is a psychologically and emotionally charged process, and the urge to make familiar meaning to avoid vulnerability is powerful. Relational supervision enhances the containment of this process. Musing on relational experiences from an artist's frame allows the bringing together of different epistemological positions, otherwise inhibited by a scientific frame, with its limitations regarding being unable to define meaningful change at a personal level, nor understand the nature of change itself with its unknowns. Also, a divergent artistic frame has within it the intention of pushing boundaries to stimulate reflection, as opposed to reciting apparent truth.

Chapter 3

Relational supervision – a two-person approach

Heather Fowlie

Relational approaches to therapy have at their core the aim of bringing a client's relational expectations into awareness, and where they limit the capacity to be open, spontaneous and intimate (Berne, 1961) the opportunity to reevaluate and transform them.

The fact that these relational expectations are for the most part unconscious means that many of the traditional therapeutic techniques that can be successfully employed to effect cognitive or behavioural change are inadequate when working with a client's deeply held relational expectations. These require, instead, an approach that allows for and promotes the experiential re-surfacing of these relational patterns within the safety and the holding of the therapeutic relationship, particularly as they are enacted between the therapeutic couple. I have described elsewhere the relational framework that involves the therapist in not only observing but actively participating in the client's relational world, being drawn into the 'many and varied aspects of these self-and-object-relationships as they occur in the process between them' (Fowlie, 2005, p. 205).

Working in this way requires a model of supervision that can both support and help the therapist to develop and deepen her capacity to enter into and engage with the many and varied aspects of the client's relational world, and to help her detach herself, if and when her own relational patterns become unhelpfully entangled with the client's.

Traditional models of TA supervision, like some of the more traditional models of TA therapy, which choose and target interventions toward achieving cognitive and behavioural level change, are unlikely to be useful in supporting a therapist to do this. These models, unlike a relational model of supervision, arise out of clinical models of therapeutic practice which have at their core very different ideas about what effective therapy is, how it should be practiced and how a clinician needs to work with their clients to achieve this.

In this way, relational clinicians need supervisors who privilege and embrace relational ways of working, some of the key features of which have been adapted from Benjamin (2002a) by Fowlie and Sills (2011) and include the following: it assumes a two-person psychology (as opposed to a one-person or one-and-a-half-person); there is an emphasis on the centrality and mutuality of the therapeutic relationship and the role it plays in change; there is an emphasis on mutual participation and engagement, with the therapist viewed as an active participant within the work; there is a considerable focus on the therapist's subjectivity as manifested via their counter-transferential reactions; it moves away from a 'parental paradigm' where the practitioner acts as a temporary provider of what was once missing for the client, and stresses instead the importance of authentic relating.

In addition, Frawley-O'Dea and Sarnat, in their seminal book on contemporary psychodynamic supervision, suggest that relational clinicians need supervisors who not only hold to a relational model in their own clinical practice, but also hold to the model in the way that they are prepared and able to offer supervision, stating that the 'medium of supervision must be consistent with the message of clinical theory' and that 'the process of supervision parallels the analytic work' (2001, p. 62).

In the light of this, they suggest three main 'dimensions' which are present in all supervisory models, but which, when adopted within a relational framework, take on a particular form that are, by their very nature, different than when they are adopted by a supervisor working within a different framework. As a way of describing and explaining the differences, I will briefly outline the main theoretical frameworks that exist within psychology today and then discuss the ways in which each of these approaches might adopt these three dimensions in their supervisory approach. The three dimensions are: the nature of the supervisor's authority in relation to the supervisee; the supervisory focus; and the supervisor's primary mode of participation.

Three different psychologies – a brief overview

One-person approach

Our ideas about the nature of the therapeutic relationship and how to use this relationship to promote healing have changed radically since Freud. His model of supervision, like most supervisory models, was informed by, and intrinsically linked to, the therapeutic model that he believed was most effective in promoting that healing, namely psychoanalysis.

Freud's clinical approach is often referred to, after Balint (1937) first coined the phrase, as a one-person psychology, a term that was developed to differentiate an approach like Freud's, with its emphasis on the internal or intrapsychic dynamics of the individual, from a two-person approach, which Balint suggested placed its emphasis instead on what occurs at an interpersonal level, or between people.

As the emphasis within a one-person model is on the internal dynamics of the individual, it is perhaps not surprising that therapists working within this model see themselves as outside of the therapeutic field, as healthy objective observers, 'blank screens' onto which the patient projects figures from the past, which they, unaffected and separate from these projections, then interpret.

Linking this stance of therapeutic separateness and objectivity to the way that a supervisor immersed in a one-person model would supervise, Frawley-O'Dea and Sarnat suggest that in terms of the supervisor's power – 'the supervisor is viewed as a neutral, objective observer of the supervisee and of the case material' (2001, p. 17). They go on to suggest that the supervisor is deemed to hold superior expert knowledge, which needs to be 'conveyed downwards' to the supervisee. As the supervisor is seen to be above enactments, difficulties within the therapy or for that matter the supervisory relationship are seen in a similar way, namely as the patient's resistance to the therapy, and the supervisee's difficulty in accepting the knowledge given by the supervisor is seen as 'a limitation of the supervisee alone' (ibid., p. 16).

In terms of the supervisory focus, in classical psychoanalysis, the therapeutic focus is on helping the client to gain knowledge and insight about themselves (particularly at the unconscious level) in the belief that this will help them to gain control over and resolve internal conflict. The supervisory focus would, therefore, be centred on helping the supervisee to understand the client's mind and ensuring that the supervisee was adhering to correct technique.

According to Aron one-person psychology transference was not 'conceptualized as an interpersonal event occurring between two people but was rather understood as a process occurring within the mind of the analysand' (1990, p. 475). It seems likely then that the supervisory focus would be exclusively targeted on the patient's transference and resistance, on the intra-psychic process and and how to treat the patient. It would exclude any discussions about the supervisee's or the supervisor's part in any enactment, other than to see this as a problem within the therapist, which requires more therapy.

Given the above, the supervisor's primary mode of participation is, therefore, didactic, someone who is viewed as an expert of technique and psychodynamics.

It seems important to state here for the sake of clarity that the above description of a supervisor working within a one-person approach does not mean that a relational supervisor would never take up a position of authority, or 'knowing best', in this way. Sometimes, particularly if a supervisee is new to client work, or a client is at risk, or a supervisee has become so entangled in a relational dynamic that they seem unable to reflect helpfully upon it, this kind of participation from the supervisor is both necessary and appropriate. The difference would come from the way in which each of supervisors is likely to reflect upon and make meaning of their intervention. For example, aware of the necessity that the supervisor felt to intervene rather more forcefully than they usually might, a relational supervisor, unlike a supervisor operating within a one-person approach, is likely to be interested in exploring and discussing with the supervisee the meaning that they both made of this and the impact of doing so on their relationship.

One-and-a-half-person approach

The one-and-a-half-person approach is a term that Morrison (1994) developed to describe a way of working that arose partly out of dissatisfaction with a classical Freudian way of viewing the mind, namely in terms of its relationship to the id, ego and superego, into one which speaks instead of the importance of the relationship.

Within this approach, the focus shifted away from insight by way of interpretation, to the provision, in the here and now, of that which the client had not received from their parents – in other words a corrective experience, at the hands of the therapist, via the meeting of relational needs – such as those espoused by Erskine (1996) and which include the need for validation, affirmation, recognition and acceptance by a stable, dependable other person.

Linking this stance of therapeutic provision to the way that a supervisor immersed in a one-and-a-half-person model might supervise, authority is likely to come from the assumption that the supervisor is more experienced than the supervisee and can, therefore, offer them support and assistance with theory and technique. Problems that arise in the therapy are mostly viewed in terms of the client's particular problems, the supervisee's inexperience or the fact that the supervisee has lost compassion for the client, which is making it difficult for them to act in a reparative way with the client.

Counter-transferential difficulties such as the above are often addressed by the supervisor under the 'restorative function' (Proctor, 1986) of supervision, with the supervisor acting as a container for the supervisee's anxieties, through empathically helping them understand their client and/or through directing the supervisee to work through what is seen to be a personal limitation in their own therapy.

In terms of the supervisory emphasis, the patient's psychology and how to understand and work with this is the primary focus – a focus which, according to Frawley-O'Dea and Sarnat, is best supported through a supervisory relationship that functions and acts as a kind of mentoring relationship. Within this framework, the supervisee is deemed to learn how to be with the client from the way that the supervisor is with them: 'the supervisee learns implicitly from the process of the supervision how to manage a helping relationship with a minimum of visible intrusion from the helper's psychology' (2001, p. 31).

Given the above, the supervisor's primary mode of participation is, therefore, didactic, supportive and mentoring, concerned with developing the skills, abilities and understandings of the supervisee/practitioner through a reflection on clinical practice and showing the supervisee how to respond to the client's material.

As noted, under a one-person model the description above is not intended to suggest that a relational supervisor ignores, for example, the development of the supervisee's skills and abilities. This kind of developmental focus is a natural and necessary component of supervision, particularly with less experienced supervisees, whatever the framework. The relational supervisor will, however, be most interested in helping the supervisee to increasingly develop those skills which will best assist them to engage openly, curiously, non-defensively and at relational depth, with the dynamics that emerge within the clinical relationship.

Two-person approach

In a two-person psychology, the approach most closely associated with relational psychotherapy, the emphasis is on what Stark (2000) refers to as 'authentic relating', in the belief that the act of experiencing and exploring what transpires between the two parties as they engage in such a relationship (or attempt to avoid it), has the potential to challenge, disrupt and transform deeply held implicit relational expectations: 'The ultimate goal is resolution of the patient/s relational difficulties and development of her capacity to engage healthily and authentically in relationship' (ibid., p. 4).

In keeping with the emphasis on authenticity and relational dynamics, it is not surprising that relational therapists seek out supervisory spaces where they will be sensitively challenged to make use of and meaning out of those times when they or the supervisor believe that their capacities for contact, curiosity and non-defensiveness are being compromised in uncharacteristic ways; as well as spaces where they will be supported to hold, contain, and symbolise powerful dynamics as they manifest within the therapeutic relationship, or conversely, find expression within the supervisory relationship.

Fiscanlani's (1997) definition of supervision as a 'relationship about a relationship about other relationships' seems to legitimise the importance of recognising the supervisory relationship as a valid and effective medium in its own right. It is a relationship that can effectively work to uncover and work with unconscious relational themes that are attempting to emerge in the work, and that need to be engaged with in order for the therapeutic work to progress, regardless of which relational pairing they parallel or originate from. This is in keeping with Frawley-O'Dea's belief that the more explicitly the supervisor and supervisee can appropriately discuss their own relationship, in particular in terms of the supervised material, the more effectively 'the supervisee can engage with the patient in identifying and speaking about the relational paradigms operating within the treatment' (2003, p. 360).

I will describe each of the three supervisory focuses in more depth in the case example below but in brief within a relational model the supervisor's authority, whilst not ignoring the greater experience that he or she usually brings to the encounter, in the main arises from her capacity to engage in, reflect upon and process the relational themes that arise within the therapeutic and/or supervisory relationships.

The supervisory focus within a relational approach is usually far less prescriptive than in the other two approaches, with all aspects of any of the participants' experience (client, supervisee, supervisor, other group supervisees) being seen as relevant and useful sources of information, when geared towards trying to understand and work through unhelpful relational patterns that are restricting and limiting the client's ability for authentic relationship. Frawley-O'Dea suggests, among other things, that the relational supervisor is 'open to considering primary-process material delivered into the supervision by dreams, somatic states, fantasies and dissociative experiences' (2003, p. 360).

Given the above, the relational supervisor may participate in a number of different ways as she or he engages in the many aspects of unconscious processes, exploring the supervisee's counter-transference, processing and exploring her own counter-transference, containing and working through difficult relational themes and providing information.

As should be apparent from the descriptions of the three different approaches outlined above, the framework on which the supervisory model is built strongly determines the way in which the supervisor interacts with the supervisee, what the supervisor deems to be appropriate material for discussion and how the supervisor sees their role.

It is not my intention to suggest that any one model is better than another; each has its strengths and weaknesses. For example one of the strengths of a one-person model is that it gives supervisees specific technical help, with a weakness being the lack of flexibility built into the model, meaning that it may not respond so well to the many and varied elements of human experience. One of the strengths of a one-and-a half-person approach is that the supervisor offers a supportive and holding relationship in which the supervisee can feel valued and supported, with a weakness resting on the potential for the supervisee to become infantilised and dependent on the supervisor. In a two-person approach, maybe its greatest strength, in terms of its flexibility to respond and make sense of the many vicissitudes of human experience, is also its greatest weakness, in that it can at times leave supervisees feeling uncertain, uncontained and longing for concrete help.

Whichever model influences the supervisor, it is my belief that in the hands of a supervisory pair who fully embrace and are ready for the model it has, no doubt, the potential to be a powerful supervisory tool, which can support the therapist to be effective and facilitative of the client's process. In the hands of a supervisory pair who are at odds with the models that they embrace, however, both parties are likely to feel frustration and experience much more powerfully, the limitations rather than the strengths that each of the models espouses, with a knock-on effect on the clinical relationships they are meant to be supporting.

As a relational clinician, I wanted a safe, supportive but also professionally challenging space that focused on unconscious processes that would support me to engage with, contain and process the difficult and strong feelings I often experienced when working with clients.

I particularly wanted a space where the kind of experiences, dynamics and processes of working relationally would be understood and assumed to be a normal and necessary part of the process rather than signs that something was wrong with the client, the work and/or myself, and which would support me in deepening my understanding and ability to work within the relational realm.

Whilst I am sadly no longer a member of one of the supervision groups upon which this book is based, due mainly to distance and problematic boundaries, I still draw upon many of my experiences and learnings that I took from it, and hold it as a model on which I base much of my own supervisory practice.

Supervision presentation

As was common practice in the supervisory group, members of the group who wished to would take it in turns to discuss their work with a client, to which the rest of the group, including the supervisor, listened and reflected upon.

After the presentation members of the group shared any associations they had had during the client presentation, often with the person who had made the presentation sitting slightly outside of the group, but still listening. This joint sharing eventually culminated in a discussion, in which the original group member joined, about how the sharing had helped them understand the relational dynamics and themes that were present in the work with the client, and, if appropriate, thoughts about how they might take this back into the work with the client.

I decided to present a client, whom I shall call Audrey

I started by giving the group some brief background information about Audrey, telling them that I had worked with her for two-and-a-half years, and that she had been sexually abused as a child by her stepfather.

I told them that this previously very talkative client had recently moved into a place in the therapy where she would sit opposite me, hardly speaking, not making eye contact and looking as if she was half asleep, and that I in contrast had begun to experience the most intense physical pain in my wrists and ankles, so much so that I wanted to cry out, feeling somehow that this would make the pain go away. Feeling uncertain, confused and trapped within some kind of silence myself, I told them that I didn't seem to be able to find a way of engaging with her about this, and was now dreading her coming to the session. I told the group that I wanted to use the time to explore the dynamics of what felt like a powerful projective identification from which I had become unable to free myself.

I began to tell the group about the two inter-related thoughts I had about what I believed could be going on. Firstly, I described how early on in our relationship we had spoken at length regarding Audrey's shame about what her stepfather had done to her, but particularly her shame about being a black client telling a white therapist, feeling that I might think that it was only black families where this happened. As a result I wondered whether these fears had resurfaced or deepened; certainly the way my client had shut down reminded me of what Minikin (2011) refers to as 'deadening passivity'. She quotes Lynch (1712), a plantation owner in Jamaica and slave consultant across the Americas to describe the origins of such passivity, which she states have been unconsciously passed down the female line for generations as a consequence of slavery. In a speech delivered in Virginia, Lynch stated that 'By her being left alone, unprotected, with male image destroyed, the ordeal caused her to move … to a frozen independent state.'

At the time, and several times through the early stages of therapy, I had responded to Audrey's reference to race with feelings of guilt for being white, but more powerfully feeling as if anything that I said or did, because of my whiteness, would somehow hurt her, and move me into what Davies and Frawley (1994) name as a 'sadistic abuser' in a relationship with a 'helpless, impotently enraged victim'. My discomfort and fear of stepping into this role, of intruding into the client's space with my own need to rid myself of pain and feelings of white guilt, conversely moved me into the victim role instead.

I didn't know, I told the group, whether from this victim role I was angry with my client, only that I knew that my attempts to make any kind of interpretation about this with my client, who had told me previously that she would pretend to be asleep when she was being abused, had not seemed to shift the dynamic. Likewise, neither had revisiting our discussions about our difference, shame or guilt helped to make any inroads.

Secondly and relatedly, I wondered whether I was experiencing something of what my client might have felt when, as a child, she was being sexually abused and pinned to the bed by the weight of the man who was abusing her. As I said this I felt as if I was beginning to lose my capacity to think and I began to slip into feeling the same intensity of physical pain that I experienced when sitting with my client. In addition I felt an extreme and previously unfelt desperation and sense of isolation and panic.

I wanted to cry out, similarly to how I felt when I was with my client. I wanted someone bigger and stronger to know about the pain – I wanted the supervisor, in particular, to know. I wanted her to take it away, but I felt the most intense shame about needing anyone, and also about the 'young', unexpected and unwanted feelings I was experiencing towards the supervisor.

I defensively tried to avoid these feelings, battling within myself to stay thinking, trying repeatedly to explain from a cognitive place what was going on, but words could not capture the depth of what I was experiencing and my shame and inability to speak without emotion, something that I felt terrified in the moment of doing seemed to make this an impossible and futile task. I could not bear it and so instead I began to shut down and as I did so I lost contact with myself, and the rest of the group. I sank into a world where pain and despair did not exist, and I floated out of the room and away from them all.

I am not really sure how long I was gone but very slowly, from somewhere deep within this dissociated place I began bit by bit to come back, to regain some contact with myself and where I was. Eventually I looked up, in an effort to ground myself, and as I did so I caught the supervisor's eye, feeling immediately overwhelmed, and instinctively looked down and retreated back inside of myself. As soon as I did so I knew that I had a choice to make. I could stay apart and hold onto the feeling of protective safety that this separateness seemed to afford me, however lonely, or I could make contact and open myself up to the possibility of being understood and accepted by another, however frightening and painful that might feel.

In the midst of my decision, I knew that whilst I was indeed experiencing a part of my client's intra-psychic and interpersonal struggle I was also right up against something that felt like part of my own struggle, and as I recognised this I knew that if I wanted to advance the work with my client I needed to face and conquer this place within myself. To look up seemed so simple, and yet at the same time it felt shameful and impossible. Somehow, by finding strength and courage I didn't know I had, I came back a little, making eye contact with the supervisor and connecting with the group again, and as I did so, I felt a freedom inside of myself, a release, as well as a deeper connection and understanding of my client.

I didn't hear too much of the group discussion that followed, as, whilst I was back, I was feeling shocked by the intensity of what I had experienced and still a little dissociated. I remember watching them talk and feeling very held by their discussion, even though I couldn't really hear their words. I felt allowed to be exactly where I was, which helped me to know at a very deep level that my client needed that time and non-intrusive attention from me too. I didn't know (and still don't) whether my reflections and feelings whilst they were talking mirrored anything that was being said, but what I took from it was that I needed to create a similar space for my client, a space where pain, suffering and dissociation could be contained and sat with, and where there was an offer of contact, but most importantly, no need in the other for it to be made.

It reminded me of the kind of space that Montross (2013) talks of, suggesting that so often we (she is talking about psychiatrists but could be talking about psychotherapists too) miss creating that kind of space because we want to distance ourselves from the person's suffering and our helplessness in the face of that. Quoting the work of W. Curt LaFrance, she talks of the need to 'abide with' clients, which she describes as a 'powerful term that embodies diligence and, importantly, inaction' (p. 179).

I had temporarily lost my ability to abide with my client. Rather than be with her, I was trying to stay separate and away from the feelings that had been stirred in me in relation to her, feelings of guilt, shame, helplessness and, particularly, a terror of letting the other in, of showing need and want for another.

Whilst the group modelled a way to create that space, this was not the most important bit for me. With a different client and even with this one at a different time, I knew how to do that. What was far more relevant was that it offered an opportunity for me to experience and then face what was preventing me from providing it, at that moment, with this client. Trapped as I was in a projective identification that had originated between my client and myself, this different setting and these different minds enabled me to free myself from the part of the projective identification that I could and was identifying with – as Wachtel says, what the client 'puts into' the therapist 'is not just a product of the patient's insides, but of the therapist's sensitivities and readiness to perceive' (2008, p. 125).

I was open to and did get caught into a powerful projective identification with this client and her with me, in some sense both of us representing for each other the 'Feared Others' (Fowlie, 2005) that permeate our narratives. For her, I was an abuser, an unavailable mother, a racist – powerful projections, which hooked both of us into a stalemate. As Aron comments, 'the feeling that we must either submit or resist is the hallmark of the doer-done to relationship' (2006, p. 351).

Our 'doer-done to' relationship – a term that originated from Benjamin (2004) – however painful, served as a potent, defensive block behind which we could both hide from the more vulnerable feelings that we shared in common: a fear of our need and desire for contact with the other.

To free myself, I needed to do the very thing that both of us found so difficult: to ask for help, to let another see my vulnerability, to reach out – thereby releasing myself to go back into the work with my client in a potentially altered relational space. Benjamin (2002a, p. 2) states that, when working relationally, 'the analyst must change, the analyst needs to surrender'. The group helped me to take the risk and surrender.

It is beyond the scope of this article to describe in depth how the supervision impacted on my work with this client, other than to say that one of the many things I felt I gained from it was help to disentangle myself from a relational dynamic I was struggling to work through. It helped me reclaim what Aron and Benjamin refer to as 'thirdness', which they describe as 'a process of identification with the patient's position without [the therapist] losing her own perspective' (1999, p. 351) – a perspective that I had lost and, subsequently, with the help of the supervision, recovered.

In the often challenging and powerful work that lay ahead with Audrey, I was able to call that supervision session to mind (along with several others that I took on the same client) and use it supportively. I was able to use the learning I took from it to stay empathic to her fear of connection and remain curious about the many, often disturbing transferential and counter-transferential positions we inhabited during our work together. Equally I used it to stay compassionate to the part of me that sometimes fears contact. Stirred by the client's wounds, I found an empathy for myself, which Shmukler refers to when she describes a two-person psychotherapy as one in which 'we discover our weaknesses and strengths and are forced to grow and develop aspects of our personalities' (1991, p. 134).

Discussion

The nature of the supervisor's authority in relationship to the supervisee

As should be evident from the way that the supervisory space described above was formulated, from the outset power was shared between the group members. This was a way of working that both accounted for the experience of the members of that particular group and fit with Frawley-O'Dea and Sarnat's (2001) ideas about the way a relational supervisor who seeks to work within a two-person model should best engage with their authority.

This is not to suggest that within a two-person model the supervisory relationship is seen as symmetrical, or that there is an attempt to remove any power differential – far from it. Like any supervisory relationship, the relational supervisor has primary responsibility for establishing and maintaining boundaries, for example, or for ensuring that both parties stay focused on the task. Within a two-person model, however, the relational supervisor adopts a stance that could be described as similar to what Holloway (1995) calls 'power with' as opposed to 'power over'. This is a stance that is less connected to a philosophical belief about power-sharing, although many relational supervisors do hold this as a belief, but instead arises out of the relational belief that reality and truth are most often perceptual, rather than factual. This suggests an approach where perceptions are, therefore, mutually explored rather than unilaterally concretised and defined by any one member of the therapeutic or supervisory dyad. In this way, the thoughts, feelings, perspectives and co-created meanings of all parties – the client, the supervisee and the supervisor – are considered, reflected upon and seen to be of value.

To accomplish this, the supervisory group, as modelled by the supervisor, start from the belief that they have no special knowledge or truth about the client (or the supervisee or the supervised work), and that, in fact, each of their own versions of the truth and reality are perceptual and limited. Therefore, and without discounting the greater experience that she brings to the exchange, or the responsibilities inherent in her role, the relational supervisor, instead of asserting what is 'true' or stating how things should be done, rather uses her own (and in this case the group's) reflections to account for, seek out, consider and explore with the supervisee the insights and meanings she identifies with (and that the client emphasises). She then trusts the supervisee to take these meanings, once they have been expanded upon, back into the work with the client, in her own particular way.

The supervisor's focus: the relevant data for supervisory processing

As can be seen from the supervisory example above, there is an acceptance of and welcoming of creative ways of presenting supervisory material. A central concept of relational therapy is an awareness of and focus on unconscious process. Translating this into the supervisory relationship, these processes, because they are repressed, dissociated and/or unsymbolised, are often difficult to put into readily understood narratives. As a result the supervisory space needs to be flexible, imaginative and safe enough to help the supervisee to present and make meaning of such material. In practice, this may mean, as was the case with the example above, being open to the supervisee presenting with regressive or dissociative experiences, somatic presentations and the use of parallel processes and projective identifications. The fact that these forms of presentations were seen as normal within the setting, and could be contained within the group, made it possible for me to allow myself to enter more fully into the client's (and my own) repressed material, so that I could fully embrace them, find meaning in them and then detach myself enough from them to be of use to my client.

As was the case in the client example above, and is so often the case, I believe, when the treatment gets stuck, some of my own primitive states were affecting my ability to maintain a 'third' position, and I was becoming instead entangled and lost under the pressure of my client's trauma-induced projections and what was being stirred in me as a result. Like other members of the group, the fact that I had undergone and remained in my own in-depth personal therapy provided both a 'known quality' to the kind of primitive experiencing I was undergoing and a willingness to explore the meaning of what had happened, in the service of better understanding the relational processes of the clinical work I was presenting.

In keeping with relational ways of working, the therapist's experience of the client and the relational patterns that emerge between them are viewed as so central in understanding and guiding the therapeutic process that the supervision cannot be effectively carried out without addressing the supervisee's counter-transferences to her client, including those bits that McLaughlin (2005) calls the therapist's transferences. In this way, a rigid demarcation between teaching and treating, or what is often referred to as the teach–treat boundary, is not only deemed to be incompatible with relational ways of working, but also seen as undesirable, and probably impossible. What seems important, and was certainly the case within the group, is that both the supervisee and supervisor are clear with each other about the purpose of any kind of exploration, or working with, the supervisee's personal experiences, and that it remains as Frawley-O'Dea and Sarnat state: 'indentured to the overarching goal of facilitation of the supervisee's growth as a clinician' (2001, p. 140).

In other words, whilst in a therapeutic relationship the purpose of working on transferences and counter-transferences is to explore, deconstruct and reconstruct the perceptual meanings and relational patterns that emerge for the client. In the supervisory relationship, the purpose of this kind of exploration is limited to encouraging, enabling and promoting effective therapeutic work. In the case example above, the fact that the group worked as an effective container of my dissociated state and the supervisor in particular offered a non-threatening but available presence, I was able to take the space to work on the part of me that deals with acute emotional discomfort through primitive withdrawal and shutdown, thereby enabling me to go back into the therapeutic space with a greater capacity to tolerate my client's primitive states.

Scharness talks of relational supervision as having both an educational and a therapeutic focus, as well as a permeable boundary between 'professional development, personal growth, and personality change' (2006, p. 428).

Whilst in my own case there was no overt exploration of what happened between myself and the supervisor, or myself and the group for that matter, as there seemed no clinical need for this discussion to take place, an exploration of the dynamics that emerge between the supervisee and supervisor is certainly not uncommon in relational supervision. What seems important here is that any such discussion about the supervisory dynamics are only done if the needs of the client and the supervised work are the primary focus and purpose of the discussion.

One of the working assumptions that underlie this is that the dynamics that emerge between the supervisory pair or between members of the supervisory group are often a rich source of information about relational processes that are attempting to emerge within the therapeutic relationship, often referred to as a parallel process (which I say more about below). This was certainly, in part, what happened in the supervision example I presented above, but to view all such dynamics as simply representative of the dynamics between the therapeutic pair is probably defensive and unhelpful.

Within a relational approach, parallel process, similarly to projective identification, is viewed as representing just one of the creative and imaginative ways in which unconscious material can find its way into consciousness. First linked to therapy by Searles, he defined parallel process as an unconscious identification with a client, in which 'processes at work currently in the relationship between patient and therapist are often reflected in the relationship between therapist and supervisor' (1955, p. 135). Whilst Searles' definition assumes that the relationship being paralleled has arisen out of the supervisee-client relationship, relational practitioners view parallel process as a natural part of all and every relationship, and accept that the parallel can, in fact, arise out of any of the dyads.

In this way, they differ from the view of parallel process as exemplified by the one-person and one-and-a-half-person supervisors, in which it represents a negative process, a stuck-ness in which they as neutral observers need to spot the process and bring it to the supervisee's attention. Rather, they accept that they may well enter into and get caught up in the enactment for a while, in that way understanding more about and being able to expand upon the multiple meanings that the original dyad (whichever dyad that might be) might be struggling to convey and work through.

In the supervision example I gave above, the parallel process does seem to have originated in the therapeutic relationship. Seeing the parallel process as the way in which the powerful projective identification that I was experiencing with my client could be brought into the supervisory space and worked with, I was provided with an opportunity to experience, process and make meaning of cut-off, unexpressed parts of myself and my client that were previously unavailable for verbal discussion and exploration. Had the supervisor or the group rushed to point this out to me, assuming that they had not entered into the enactment themselves (although interestingly rushing into making early cognitive sense of the experience may well have been a different kind of projective identification), it is unlikely that I would have had the profound and experiential learning that I did. Mendelsohn concurs with this when he suggests that simply pointing out the presence of a parallel process 'adds no new information to the supervision', but that 'an exploration of the parallel enactments' between all of the relevant parties 'can enrich the treatment, as well as the supervision' (2012, p. 297).

The supervisor's primary mode of participation

The relational supervisor and the relational group engage in the supervisory relationship in a range of ways, most of which are designed to assist exploration of the unconscious processes of the various participants involved in the work, including the supervisor's, and to explore and work through the inevitable enactments that typify the therapeutic and supervisory work. As Frawley-O'Dea and Sarnat state, 'This is a highly experiential approach to teaching and learning' (2001, p. 41).

There seems little more to say here in relation to this heading, only that I hope I have shown in this chapter some of the ways in which the supervisor and the supervisory group participated in my exploration of the clinical work that I brought to the group. Whilst never overtly spoken about on this occasion with the group or the supervisor, or used openly in dialogue with the client, the supervisory experience had a profound affect on me and worked as a release that allowed, or perhaps modelled, a similar shift in my client.

Conclusion

The relational supervision group provided me with a space in which, because I felt safe and supported, I could allow myself to enter into and explore away from the client (to whom I had a different responsibility) the full extent of what was going on inside of me in relation to her. The feeling of safety I felt was supported by three things. Firstly I knew that everyone in that room would have experienced their own versions of what I was experiencing, and in fact I had witnessed them doing so. Secondly I knew that we all subscribed to a way of viewing psychotherapy as a relational encounter where, as well as observing the client's relational world, we must be willing to enter into and engage with it, and that we all accepted that an inevitable and healthy part of this is that primitive processes within ourselves would get stirred. Lastly, what I was feeling and experiencing was supported in the relational literature. For example Benjamin (2009, p. 441) talks about the 'inevitability of enactments and impasses', and Gill suggests that the therapist alternates between periods of 'unwitting enactment' into which the therapist falls and 'witting interpretation' of such enactment (1987, p. 259).

The fact that I shared some defensive similarities to my client meant that instead of being able to enter my client's relational world and then reclaim an 'observational space', I was both resisting entering her world and at the same time getting very entangled in it. My ability to make sense of what was happening had become compromised. The group provided me with the strength and courage to go into the part of my client's world that I was scared to enter, and to then detach from the experience enough to reclaim the observational space that I needed to allow the treatment to progress.

Benjamin (2002a, p. 2) states that when working relationally 'the analyst must change, the analyst needs to surrender'. The group helped me to surrender, and I was then free to help my client to risk the same.

Chapter 4

Take this to therapy?

Birgitta Heiller

Many years ago, just after being endorsed as a 'provisional' supervisor, I sat in front of a group of trainee psychotherapists who worked for a newly established low-cost service at their place of training, pens poised. I was a fledgling, and as anxious as they were. I realised that anything that dropped from my lips would be seen as coming 'from the horse's mouth', and indeed, whenever I uttered any musings, they were eagerly recorded. I went home, terrified. I had passed all the criteria for being a budding supervisor, but felt that I knew nothing, and had to find my own way forward. I soon came to the conclusion that I would never want to be seen as 'the expert' on anything. The potential for idolisation, or 'projective transference' (Hargaden and Sills, 2002), was great, with the associated subsequent fall from grace a definite risk, and almost impossible to avoid. But how was I to divest myself from the projection, or indeed work with it? Somehow I had got my head around that as a psychotherapist (or at least so I thought), but the status of 'supervisor' that had been newly conferred upon me opened up a different vista, both daunting as well as liberating. At the same time, I somehow knew that I was there to impart something important to those students, to be an object of their introjective transferences (ibid., 2002). That book hadn't been written at the time, so it was difficult for me to know what was what. I had to find my own style, and a group I joined some years later was invaluable in that regard.

My experience in a relational supervision group

About five years after that first experience I decided to join a relational supervision group exploring clinical issues based solely on unconscious processes. About once a month, a whole day was devoted to open exploration and mutual learning without any judgment. Concurrently, I was readying myself for an exam to confirm my status as a fully qualified supervisor and trainer. At this stage in my professional development, where at least some certainty about the process of therapy and purpose of supervision was expected, the group offered a welcome, if somewhat disconcerting, forum that allowed for ambivalence and doubt (see Stuthridge, 2011). Accounting for, and actively experiencing, strong emotions like terror, envy, rage or erotic tension was actively encouraged, and this didn't stop at the exploration of the experience between a therapist and her client. What happened between supervisor and supervisees, as well as between group members, was equally important. Acute and often unpleasant feelings in response to a client presentation, to an exchange between colleagues or to the reaction of the group facilitator were actively endorsed. It was the epitome of what Berne referred to as 'intimacy' (Berne, 1964), with all its associated hazards as well as benefits.

Preparing for the exam to become a fully qualified trainer and supervisor was an ongoing challenge in the first two years of my attendance in the group. This "TSTA" exam process necessitated adherence to stringent criteria and a sense of command and certainty both in teaching as well as in supervision, and often my experience in the relational supervision group was perplexing and unsettling. What was I now supposed to teach my students, or direct my supervisees towards, especially the beginners, if I were to embrace the type of uncertainty that emerges when we engage with unconscious processes? When in the group, I was coming to grips with opening up an expanse of different meaning-making, and purposely allowing for ambiguity and the need to stay with it. When teaching my students, I reckoned that I had to supply them with certainties to hold on to. Many supervisees also justifiably expected some guidance with regard to practice, and how to utilise theoretical models in a way that would eventually lead towards a quantifiable outcome. After all, they needed to demonstrate their effectiveness as TA therapists in exams, and the same was the case for me as supervisor and trainer. I felt torn.

Early experiences in the group

When I decided to join the group, I did not realise how challenging this gradual transformation of my perception of myself as a therapist and possibly even more so, as a supervisor and trainer would prove to be. I regularly felt emotionally drained and tired at the end of a day. I found the discrepancy between what I had been taught and what I thought I ought to teach at times too vast to deal with.

After passing the exam two years later, those feelings changed. It was almost as though I had only then joined the group 'for real', being released from the confines of what I had until then considered to be the parameters of my job. In some ways, I had been no different from those fledgling supervisees years ago, who had been looking for answers from me, and providing them with 'the truth'. Paradoxically, I felt more comfortable being vulnerable as a qualified trainer and supervisor. Something similar had happened when I passed the exam to qualify as a clinical practitioner eight years prior – it freed me up to explore other avenues, while being officially endorsed by my 'certified' status.

An important experience occurred at the end of my first year, when one of the original group members left. It was a slow and painful experience to watch both supervisor and supervisee struggle with strong emotions, and the relief and release when the two came to a point where they could part from each other. While this process has a different relevance in a supervisory connection, the principle is the same as in relational psychotherapy. It involves two people, sometimes in the presence of other members of a group, who have to work through difficult feelings together. At the end of the day, no one knows more than the other. No one is 'inviting the other into a game', but they are both involved in some dynamic together (Hine, 1990; Summers and Tudor, 2000; Tudor and Summers, 2014; Stuthridge, 2015). It takes courage and honesty to be with others in this way, and to refrain from calling it transference/counter-transference (McLaughlin, 2005), thereby departing from psychoanalytic, or any other, orthodoxy. I started thinking about the implications of this – what needs to be 'taken to therapy' (as the time-honoured advice goes) and what can, and indeed needs to be, dealt with in the supervisory relationship itself? This is something I am also more and more mindful of as a therapist to both trainee as well as qualified practitioners. It is all very well to discuss transferential issues in one's own psychotherapy, but more often than not they reside in the co-created relationship between supervisor and supervisee, and hence need to be resolved there. This requires a commitment to an honest appraisal of the situation by both parties.

A clinical example

In the following example I want to illustrate the perceptive powers of the relational supervision group and the difficulty I experienced on occasion in making sense of other group members' responses to a client presentation.

Fairly early on, I brought a new client to the group, whom I had only seen for two sessions at the time. She was signed off work with stress and, during the initial interview, she recounted a lifetime of abuse and neglect, and a tendency to blame herself for everything. She was in an emotionally, and at times physically, abusive relationship. I felt deep compassion and got very involved in her story. In the second session she spoke of her grief around not having been the mother she had wanted to be for her children, and again I felt tearful and conveyed to her how moved I felt. Unaware that I was locked in a provisional mode, a one-and-a-half-person model (Stark, 1999) of doing therapy, it disturbed and confounded me that she rejected any expression of empathy and wanted to leave the session early. When I presented the client in the group, the other members' responses 'threw' me. They experienced boredom, annoyance, even the urge to ridicule the person. The word 'pathetic' was used. I felt deeply offended and hurt on her behalf, as well as on my own, even personally attacked by the 'unempathic' response. I had virtually 'acted' the client, so deeply had I got embroiled in her narrative and what I saw as her predicament, and all I was left with was confusion.

Over the next weeks, I found myself wanting to dismiss the responses the group had had towards this woman, and got ever more immersed in her story. However, whenever I conveyed my empathy directly, she fended me off vigorously, and started calling herself pathetic (just as the group had felt her to be) and stupid. I hadn't made the connection immediately, but after some weeks of this self-flagellation I began feeling annoyed and bored with her, exactly the feelings that my colleagues had experienced when I had presented her after only two sessions.

The feelings that the group members seemed to have picked up at the time reflected her self-loathing and habitual putting down of herself, as well as anticipating the response of people around her, including myself, when exposed to her constant self-abasement and rejection of positive and encouraging responses. In fact, as it transpired, a previous therapist at one point threw her out during a session, and later discontinued work with her abruptly altogether. The client had managed to manoevre herself into a position that confirmed her basic beliefs about herself.

As a result of reflecting on the process in the group I changed my way of working and stopped conveying empathy verbally. This runs counter to the notion of a 'stroke-centered' therapy, with strokes being defined as 'transactional units of recognition' (Steiner, 2003, p. 178), or indeed the attempt at meeting relational needs (Erskine et al., 1999) but it seemed to suit this client much better, at least at that point, and I no longer felt rebuffed. I also felt less drawn into the story, while remaining emotionally deeply involved and often unsettled. I monitored my own responses more closely. I sometimes experienced a level of fear, which told me about another important aspect of her experience, and possibly others' experience of her. I refrained from emotional self-disclosure, keeping these feelings to myself, only quietly noting them. In doing so, I endeavoured to avoid a situation such as Benjamin describes: 'I, as bystander, could fail her, cause pain in seeing her too positively … allying my ideal self with her "good" self, leaving her "bad" self shamed and excluded' (2009, p. 445). Benjamin continues, 'By failing to grasp how desperate her plight was … I was occluding her shameful, monster self' (ibid., p. 445). Despite the fact that the therapy with this client didn't end according to plan, I hope she did ultimately feel more 'seen' by me in her self-loathing and hatred, and maybe that was an experience she hadn't had in the past and one which she could ultimately benefit from.

Discussion

The 'route of transmission' of these unconscious ways of picking up things remains somewhat elusive, despite the fact that it has been phenomenologically described in various ways. In transactional analysis, Berne's initial studies on intuition (1977) come to mind, as well as the concept of projective identification (Klein, 1946; Bion, 1962; Ogden, 1982/1992). Hargaden and Sills (2002) term it 'transformational' transference. Schore (2003/2012) describes the right-brain to right-brain connection which bypasses the conscious processing in, chiefly, the left hemisphere. Beebe and Lachmann (2003) speak of mutual affect regulation, Stern *et al.* (1998) of implicit relational knowing, and relational analysts generally term it bi-directionality of the relational unconscious (Hargaden and Schwartz, 2007). Curiously, though, in the above case the responses occurred not in the client-therapist encounter, but rather during a case presentation when the client was not present. This phenomenon is an essential aspect of the Balint-style group (Hargaden, this book), and has also been described by Sletvold (2014) as embodied reflexivity, a version of the 'third' (see later). When I first encountered it, however, it was perplexing.

For the purpose of this chapter I won't go into any more detail about the actual work with the client, chiefly wishing to highlight the dynamic of the powers of the unconscious of the assembled supervision group and their bearing on how I changed my approach.

Challenges

Despite feeling freed after having achieved my teaching and supervising qualifications, to an extent I continued to struggle with some aspects of the relational approach to my core modality, as it was gradually formulated. Probably still on some level seeking a new 'clear' direction, I was thrown off balance. Transactional analysts, as well as other humanistic therapists, had long prided themselves as being relational, so what was this new 'wave' supposed to be? At least that is what students and supervisees alike asked me, and secretly I was asking it myself.

More often than not, the writings of relational analysts (Mitchell and Aron, 1999; Aron and Harris, 2005; Davies, 2004) or other relevant psychoanalytic authors, as well as some from the emergent tradition of relational TA (Hargaden and Sills, 2002; Cornell and Hargaden, eds, 2005; Fowlie and Sills, eds, 2011) focused on the difficult, hidden, unmanageable, frightening, perplexing and seemingly impossible feelings and impulses of both therapist and client. Primitive processes were the prime focus of attention. The willingness and ability to see the absurdity of situations, of the predicament of the human condition, in the way that these are addressed in, for example, existential psychotherapy (van Deurzen and Arnold-Baker, eds, 2005; Cohn, 1997; Yalom, 2002), seemed less often in the spotlight, at least for my liking. There is a great deal of interface between the two theoretical orientations, though the style of writing is often very different, and has different foci. As Hargaden states in the introduction to this book, 'within the humanistic modality the relational approach has involved a more intense focus on the depth of the intra-psychic and relational unconscious' (p. 4). Sometimes this seemed to be at odds with how I saw the process of therapy myself. I had to remind myself on many occasions that, again, I had to feel my own way forward and sift what seemed 'right' for me, what was a 'good fit' theoretically, and what I had to discard.

Partly in an attempt (for myself at least) to bring two strands together, I co-authored (Heiller and Sills, 2010) a chapter on the subject of existentialism and the TA theory of life scripts (Erskine, ed., 2010), and the importance of being aware of existential realities for both therapist and client. However, existentialist thought is also evolving. Recently, Loewenthal suggested that 'a post-existential perspective has more in common ... with relational psychoanalysis, psychotherapy and counselling' (2014, p. 140). To quote Loewenthal, 'what needs to be stressed is that, if we really start with practice, and see that this is what Freud and others discovered first, and only later attempted to put theories to, then all theory ... will always only have implications and not applications' (ibid., p. 142).

In many ways, my early struggles seem to be reflected in the writing of authors who are currently emerging from various theoretical 'corners' of the profession. While the tendency of psychoanalysts steeped in the tradition to gradually modify their style from interpretation to 'being with' a patient seemed clear enough (at least as seen from the outside), it was less clear to a humanistic-integrative practitioner what constituted a 'relational turn'. Some argued that a 'relational turn' in TA, or any humanistic approach, was a contradiction in terms. Often I encountered surprised, and slightly dismissive, responses from 'traditional' TA colleagues, stating that 'We have always been relational, focused on the relationship, haven't we?' This was recently echoed by Samuels:

> If I were a humanistic therapist still, I'd be feeling aggrieved. For the relational turn in psychotherapy stems from the work of Carl Rogers and the person-centred approach [Rogers, 1996]. What has been 'invented' in the United States could be termed 'humanistic psychoanalysis'.
>
> (Samuels 2014, p. 184)

Between these two opposing views, a synthesis will gradually emerge, and it probably has to be very subjective and might be different for every practitioner and theorist.

'Use of the self' – who am I?

It took me a while to be able to pinpoint what the difference was. The 'use of the self' was to become more clearly defined in the 'relational turn', in the psychoanalytic as well as the humanistic fields. Paying close attention to counter-transference responses, including bodily ones (see e.g. Sletvold, 2014, and Cornell, 2015), reflecting on our own 'script', or 'past us' (Summers and Tudor, 2000, and Tudor and Summers, 2014) were an essential part of this. I had thought I knew who I was. After all, I had been in therapy, on and off, since my early thirties, which, poignantly, I originally chiefly came to with the question 'Who am I?' However, for many years I had not 'had the time', felt the need to, could justify the expense of, and any other possible excuse I could find, for engaging in another therapeutic relationship. Probably quite out of awareness I was also trapped in a mindset that suggested that, having arrived at the 'top' of my professional hierarchy, I should not 'need it anymore'. Somehow, the old Freudian notion of 'having been fully analysed' seemed to have contributed to this. Was a 'Kontrollanalyse' (Bass, 2014; Kovács, 1935) in order, and what did that mean for my identity as a professional? This was never a consciously formulated thought, but it must have played a role. And, as Bass (2014) describes, could such a process be dealt with within the supervisory relationship or did it need a separate practitioner?

Ferenczi would have disagreed (see, for example, Ferenczi, 1988), but on the suggestion of the group facilitator, I sought out a new therapist who came from a very different theoretical background. Our paths would have never normally crossed, so boundary issues didn't arise. My therapist, whilst 'old school' Jungian, and hide-bound by her traditional training, turned out to be human, first and foremost. She sometimes said, in an almost pained way, 'I can't answer that question.' In this I recognised my own struggle. I often talked to her about my own dilemmas, be those as a therapist, supervisee, supervisor, writer or journal editor. In all those roles I felt I had to 'get it right', and 'play by the rules'. It took me a very long time to really engage, and trust. But it didn't take me long to leave the relational supervision group – I realised that I had used it, to some extent, as a therapy group. It taught me a lot about myself, and it was a very painful process, just like my original TA group therapy experience had been. However, I was in need of a one-to-one relationship – not to have a 'corrective experience', where needs were met that weren't met in the past, which by then I understood wasn't really possible, but to have a different encounter with another human being, who was sometimes frustrating (and also frustrated), sometimes withholding and sometimes simply human. While still rule-bound to an extent, when after a traumatic bereavement my therapist had to take several weeks off work, our reconnection was deeply moving, and it heralded a new phase in the work.

Reflecting on this most recent period of therapy (my fourth in total) I am even more acutely aware of the dilemmas faced by relational therapists. For humanistic folk, self-disclosure was, for a long time, part of being 'real' – I learned about my first ever therapist's relationship history in the assessment session. While the 'relational turn' in the humanistic field has led to a greater minding of boundaries and a cautiousness around revealing personal material, in some psychoanalytic circles 'there is a common misperception that to work relationally means to self-disclose relentlessly' (Wachtel, 2008, p. 245, as quoted in Little, 2011). Little (p. 50) goes on to quote Aron (1996), who invites practitioners to 'think for which clients it might be useful, at what point, and under what conditions'. I experienced my therapist relaxing into our relationship as the years passed, in the same way as I was relaxing and yielding into it myself. Maroda (2004) describes in detail the dilemma of the 'impossible distinction' between the 'real' relationship versus the transference and counter-transference. The thing I resented most at the beginning of therapy was any attempt at a 'here-and-now transference interpretation'. I went along with it at first to humour her, later started to balk at it, yet later tended to tease her with it, but also conceded to consider any potential relevance. It ended up becoming a standing joke between us, with sometimes me taking the lead.

An experiment to work on the couch for a year led to a strange sense of 'disconnect', and the decision to work face to face again was like being reunited with a lost friend or family member. I realised that I needed the mirroring (Kohut, 1971) and the sense of safety that comes with reading facial expressions. Paradoxically, at the same time I felt drawn to experimenting with clients in my own practice to work with them lying back in a recliner chair with eyes closed, which suited some of them. Working in a variety of ways freed me up in my own work, and it also highlighted for me what level of self-revelation I was comfortable with, and with whom. This most recent experience in therapy has enriched me both personally as well as professionally, and I again came to the conclusion that, professionally, I learn as much in therapy as I do in some supervision settings, with relational supervision being both a conceptual as well as an experiential bridge between the two.

A relational lens – my own style

Many years have passed since I first reflected on my experiences in the group. Casting back my mind, I sometimes found it difficult to reconcile the work I did in other modalities with what I thought was 'the new way forward'. A potential split was emerging. Debates raged in online discussion groups about whether one can work both 'with' as well as 'within' the transference (for a recent discussion, see Little, 2006). Some of my colleagues chose to work solely in one paradigm, whereas I used other approaches as well, which were seemingly incompatible – drawing, for example, on the energy psychology methods (e.g. Mollon, 2008), or later EMDR (Eye Movement Desensitization and Reprocessing) (Shapiro, ed., 2002) for short-term work, especially with trauma patients. Thankfully, the need to focus on the relational is now recognised also in some of those alternative approaches (e.g. Dworkin, 2005), much of which got published after I was no longer a member of the group. Being on the periphery, or 'straddling gaps', is a position I learned to assume very early, and it informed my own 'script'. To begin with, I thought I had to adhere to one style rather that the other. Nowadays I quite enjoy being in a position of 'respected marginality', a term Petriglieri (2007) used to locate transactional analysis within the wider field of the psychological therapies. However, in the direct encounter with individuals I often found this hard, be that in a therapeutic or a supervision setting.

On the theoretical level, I continue to be fascinated and challenged by the variety of choices we have as therapists. What should the focus be – on the life-affirming, resourceful aspects of every person, or the deepest, most primitive, potentially destructive urges and feelings? The founder of trans-actional analysis, Eric Berne, was torn between the ego psychology in the USA (which Aron in 2013 called a 'manic defence' against the Holocaust), which his two training analysts, Paul Federn and Erik Erikson, both refu-gees from Europe, were espousing, and following the flow of the humanistic movement which focused on growth, opportunities and options, while being deeply rooted in European existential philosophy and its inherent bleakness.

Over the years, I gradually assembled the disjointed elements of my experi-ence in the relational group, both in my clinical as well as my supervision practice. It helped that I had also discontinued providing regular training. Generally speaking, I felt more freed up to do my own thing and pursue my own style. During my presence in the group I gradually felt more engaged and less challenged in terms of how to combine the disparate sources I drew on for my work with clients. But still it was often hard. I struggled to combine, for example, energy psychology methods (see Mollon, 2008) with a relational stance, and on one occasion sent a traumatised client to a different practi-tioner for 'that sort of work', while continuing to see the person for 'regular' psychotherapy. I was strongly challenged when I spoke of this in the group. Why wasn't I able to combine the two, was the implication. I struggled to understand, at first assuming that I had done something wrong in even sug-gesting that the client seek out a different practitioner for her severe symp-toms. Somehow I thought I should have provided everything that the client required simply by being present and available, in a relational two-person mode (Stark, 1999).

Deploying a method, I thought, would have left that paradigm behind, deploying a one-person psychology focused on symptom relief.

It took me years to understand that, even while using new facilitative approaches – especially for the treatment of trauma, for example EMDR (Shapiro, 2002), sensorimotor work (Ogden and Minton, 2008), somatic experiencing (Levine, 2010) or even 'mindfulness' (e.g. Zinn and Thich Nat Hanh, 2009) – I could work within the relational realm, and not divert from the overall paradigm of a two-person approach, or relinquish a relational 'lens'.

The concurrent gradual professionalisation of psychotherapy, and the debate about state regulation in the UK, did not help in that regard. The 'doer and done to' (Benjamin, 2004) paradigm gradually took hold and, while statutory regulation was at least temporarily avoided, it became increasingly difficult to assert a stance that did not claim to be evidence-based.

While I struggled within myself with regard to what the 'right' thing to do was (a stance I detested in politicians, while clearly being subjected to it within my own intra-psychic world), I publicly opposed it in several ways. When I learnt more about the development of relational psychoanalysis and spoke to and heard of, various proponents, I realised that they too had similar struggles, and that everyone in the end had to find their own style of being a therapist (Bregman Ehrenberg, 2014), whatever their 'school' required of them.

An example from my supervision practice

Being part of the relational supervision group for several years not only changed me as a therapist, but also very much as a supervisor. In some ways, this was the more dramatic change, which was also noted by my existing supervisees. The following is an example of how 'not knowing' temporarily became my own creed, which was as rigid and unhelpful as the 'knowing'.

Rebecca came to me on the recommendation of her training institute. She expected, quite reasonably, for me to give her guidance with regard to how best to respond to her clients. She diligently presented case material in recorded form. The question she asked on many occasions was – what is the right intervention here? I tended to dodge this, stating that there were many potential interventions at any given point, which made her distinctly uncomfortable. We worked well, on the surface, both individually as well as in a group, but throughout we maintained a slightly uneasy relationship. Ultimately, Rebecca needed to pass a process of certification, which I helped her through. After this benchmark was reached we parted, and said good-bye. My words at the time seemed to have come unexpectedly, because I was truly sad to see her go. She stated that she thought I had never much liked her, and that she was surprised at my response.

Discussion

For relationality to fully follow through according to its own principles, we need to look at our therapeutic approaches, their corresponding theories, and the dynamics between them, as manifestations of internal object relations – in ourselves, in our practitioner communities and in our clients. There is no such thing as an idea of a therapeutic approach that is free from our fantasies – fantasies which we (and everybody else) project into them – like an ethnologist projecting their unconscious into the tribe they are studying. Taking relationality into the system would mean seeing the conflicts and splits between our approaches and traditions as parallel processes with the dynamics in the client's psyche and our own.

(M. Soth, personal communication, July 2014)

In transactional analysis, for example, we are faced with a divergence of theoretical constructs and, more importantly, 'technicalities' (Berne 2001; Drego, 1983) which probably originated in an internal split within the 'euhemerus' (Solomon, 2010; Heathcote, 2010). This idea is similar to the notion of organisational scripts (Clarkson, 1995). Even though Aron argues that 'relational psychoanalysis (and for that read, any off-shoot) may well be the first school … that did not develop around a single innovator' (2014, p. 98), there is a tendency to espouse either/or thinking.

The polarities of certainty versus uncertainty, speed versus gradual revelation, knowing versus not knowing, short-term versus long-term therapy, 'one-session cure' versus therapy several times a week, etc., are all aspects of this split between internal objects.

The division of TA training organisations (a fairly recent event in the UK, a much earlier one in other countries) is the systemic/organisational manifestation of this. Similar splits have of course happened within the psychoanalytic world, and go back as far as the early part of the twentieth century, as different groups in various countries emerged who emphasised different aspects of both technique and theory.

Rebecca trained at a place that represented one end of the polarity, while another group member was at a different training establishment which represented the other. A third member was integratively trained. While the group members really appreciated one another as persons and took great interest in, and showed empathy with, their respective personal lives, when it came to case discussions, the discomfort of their divergent viewpoints was palpable. As their supervisor, I had to hold the tension while staying true to my own theoretical leanings and approach as to the technicalities of how to conduct therapy. In fact, Rebecca and her colleague represented a split within myself – having started in what is referred to as the classical mode of transactional analysis nearly thirty years ago, I had gradually morphed into someone more partial to the relational turn, through the influence of my own supervision, reading and writing. Rebecca's need for certainty and her anxiety when she was unable to pinpoint 'what exactly was going on' or 'what the best intervention was supposed to be' was an uncomfortable reminder of my own early struggles. Something similar was described evocatively by Stuthridge (2011), who in turn gently questioned the elevation of uncertainty to being the new 'holy grail', quoting Mitchell (1993,

p. 43), 'it now sometimes appears that the capacity to contain the dread of not knowing is a measure of analytic virtue; the fewer convictions the better and braver!' I need to emphasise here that a relational approach does not in itself imply an unequivocal celebration of uncertainty, but a multiplicity of meaning is encouraged. In myself, however, this temporarily turned into a new creed.

When it comes to the evaluative tasks of supervision and guiding of a supervisee towards certification, any tensions become more poignant. In both the written as well as the oral part of psychotherapy exams a sense of certainty must prevail, an assurance that what a candidate did in a session, and how they conceptualised a case theoretically, has to hold up to scrutiny when being assessed according to stringent criteria.

In traditional psychoanalysis, the training analyst knew the candidate well and was able to deem them fit to be fully qualified, though in a fairly subjective way. While the notion of primary supervisor in TA is somewhat akin to (and probably a legacy of) this dual role, today's codes of ethics demand a separation of supervision and therapy. This brought about a dilemma – what to take to therapy and what to supervision, let alone where to take issues that arise in the supervisory relationship. A need for a clear boundary emerged over the years, and the appeal was to 'take this to therapy!' However, transference issues within the supervisory relationships are rife, if only for the many educational traumas students have often experienced. The humanistic supervisor (and tutor) is often seen as a better object than a previous 'stern teacher', until it comes to endorsing a piece of written work or a recording to be presented at an oral exam.

In the case of Rebecca and myself, while we navigated these choppy waters reasonably well, an opportunity was missed. She never spoke of her fear that I didn't like her, and I never clarified that my misgivings about the approach she was taught was going against the grain of what I believed to be the current relational wisdom. We were both hide-bound, she by the teaching at her chosen training establishment (or what she took from it) and I by my newfound creed of putting uncertainty at the heart of what therapy is all about. We were both right, and we were both wrong, and for some reason we never managed to address this. We never found a joint 'third' (see below).

In terms of the split mentioned above, we were both almost typecast in one position and the other. When I felt that something could be more certain and incisive, I upheld the conviction that I needed to endorse the ambivalent and tentative, which was probably unfair, and confusing for Rebecca. There might well have been times when she was uncertain, but was drawn to 'needing to know' because the other had become 'my polarity'. Dialectically speaking, we remained stuck in thesis and antithesis, without arriving at a synthesis which could have led to new and more interesting developments.

Some thoughts on 'the third'

The task of the supervisory couple could be seen in terms of what has become known as the third (e.g. Ogden, 1994; Benjamin, 2004). There are several interpretations of the term, and Benjamin distinguishes between a primordial third, a symbolic third and a moral third (2009). The latter could help to shed light on the evaluative task of the supervisor which gets tested when supervisee's and supervisor's views diverge. A co-created shared view of the task at hand needs to be established in order for effective work to continue. Aron (1999) poses that 'Theory functions as an expression of the Third' (p. 5), and hence it would be helpful if supervisee and supervisor agree at least to an extent on the theories they both accept as givens, and which ones they are willing to play with. Aron quotes Kaplan (in Aron, 1999, p. 6, personal communication), his supervisor at the time, stating that 'he always thought of the clinical situation as an oedipal triangle – the patient, the analyst, and the profession to which the analyst is married'. It could be argued that this is even more relevant in the supervisory relationship. But caution is in order. Benjamin (2004) thought it important 'not to reify the third, but to consider it primarily as a principle, function or relationship, rather than as a "thing" in the way that theory or rules of techniques are things' (p. 7). When evaluation is involved, the supervisory third can be in danger of being reified, but at the same time there is a need for something to hold on to. In Aron's (1999) view, 'the Third keeps the analytic situation from degenerating into nothing but a personal encounter, and a regressive one at that' (p. 5). Juxtapose this with Hargaden's statement in her introduction that we do not help people with theories, 'but with ourselves and who we are as people', and we have a dialectical tension that each therapeutic and indeed supervisory couple will have to attend to in their own unique way.

Take this to therapy!

During my reflections on my experiences spanning more than a decade, one question remains for me: what to take to therapy and what to sort out in the supervisory relationship. Relational supervision is becoming an increasing topic of interest (Yellin, 2014; Sarnat, 2014); my own experience showed that the transference/counter-transference matrix is equally present – though it is not always possible to resolve all personal issues there. Where the boundaries lie, and when things have to be taken to therapy, as the traditional admonishment suggests, is unclear, and will continue to be a source of potential conflict. The evaluative task of supervision, especially when it comes to students prior to their qualification, necessitates a certain amount of distance. My unhelpful stance towards Rebecca was ill-informed and as entrenched as the 'We need to always know what to do' position. In the meantime, I have hopefully mostly come to find a way to navigate between a student's need for guidance and their legitimate right to be shown a way forward that will enable them to pass exams, and pass them well, and offering them prospective scope for leeway, and flexibility to 'play' (Winnicott, 1971) with concepts, theories and approaches, and allow them to develop their own style. At times, the transference and counter-transference issue will have to be discussed, especially where evaluation is concerned. I have become more relaxed as far as my reluctance to self-disclose in supervision is concerned. With senior supervisees, this is less of a problem, but even there I am sometimes confronted with situations that require difficult decisions. Because of the hierarchical structure of most psychotherapy training, the 'needing to know' and giving guidance in problematic circumstances, for example when it comes to ethical dilemmas, persists. It is then often tricky to sort out what's what, what to advise a supervisee to take to their own personal therapy and what needs to be addressed in the relationship. And even when someone is fully qualified, registered, approved, chartered or whatever the case may be, the transference/counter-transference matrix applies to all relationships, and so the journey of exploration continues.

Coda

It has been twelve years since I joined the relational supervision group and, upon reflection, it was as difficult as it was rewarding. I had to free myself to find my own way forward, supported by my own therapy and subsequent very diverse supervision experiences, having left the group after about seven years. I have learnt a lot from my own supervisees, and clients who are therapists in training, as well as those who would never know much about what happens behind the scenes, and what informs my work. I thank all of them.

Chapter 5

Daring to be seen in the struggle to bring my self into relationship

Gina Sweeting

Originally trained as an integrative counsellor, my professional journey has brought me into the realm of relational theory, where I have embarked on a voyage of discovery about what it means to work within the relationship. I begin with a review of the relational theory which I have found most compatible and useful to me as a clinician. I draw on the myth of Echo and Narcissus to describe my experience of struggle and finding containment in a relational supervision group. From this process I demonstrate how I learned to bring my autonomous self into relationship with colleagues and to be more available as a therapist for a mutually influencing relationship, in the service of the client.

Relational theory

In order for the therapist to bring themselves into relationship they must have a robust-enough core self that can 'identify his or her own individuative wishes' and, when appropriate, 'to express them in reality', and be aware enough 'to defend them when under attack' (Masterson and Lieberman, 2004, p. 24). This capacity in the therapist is dependent on responsive and sensitive interpersonal experiences in early life, for out of early self-object relations grows the core self; out of oneness grows the capacity to differentiate. It is assumed that since most therapists have wounds related to this experience they are required to have therapy so that they know their internal object relational world more fully.

The relational approach involves a dialectic relationship between the self as individual and the self that exists through relationship. Stark famously described three modes of relatedness (see Chapter 3 for a fuller account of Stark's work). Briefly here I describe one- and two-person modes as follows. In a one-person relationship there can only be an accommodation of one mind, as in the following examples: the therapist may be a need-gratifying object (Bromberg,

1983) or a self-object that provides a mirror or idealised image (Kohut and Wolf, 1978). All of these are ways through which the client can feel safe and develop a sense of self. In this relational paradigm the self is an individual, autonomous and separate entity. The client either relates to the therapist as an extension of self or as someone entirely separate. In the two-person approach (Stark, 1999), where the space between client and therapist becomes the focus of therapy, the relationship becomes a living phenomenological intersubjective experience through which both therapist and client learn about, and shape, a self that is ultimately impacted by the other.

Kohut and the healthy development of self

Kohut described the child's need for mirroring, idealisation and twinship, where the caregiver provides a function for the infant that has not yet been established. He described self-objects as 'objects which we experience as part of our self' (Kohut and Wolf, 1978, p. 414). Early relationships are characterised largely by the unformed self and the caregiver as self-object. Kohut and Wolf (ibid.) argued that our self-object needs continue throughout the lifespan. As adults we all have areas of self that are unformed, so every encounter harbours our need to find validation in others that enables our potential to be fulfilled. It is for the unknown parts of self that we may well carry narcissistic needs to find our own image mirrored in the eyes of others. However, Kohut and Wolf differentiated between 'reliance on fantasies of merger with idealised and omnipotent selfobjects, or of an imperative need for perfect mirroring' (Mollon, 2001, p. 223) and the person's capacity to evoke mature object relations in search of validation. Where dependency needs have been met well enough each person within a relationship will feel free to act independently from self-object transference projections (Symington, 1983).

Complementarity

Where dependency needs for mirroring and idealisation have not been successfully navigated a relational template of dependency is inevitable, making necessary coercion or 'recruitment' (Joseph, 1989) of the other into a predictable self-object relational configuration. This can manifest in what Cassorla (2001) named 'chronic enactment', where therapist and client are pulled into complementary roles. Vulnerability, dependency, uncertainty, loss and relationship, all relational aspects of being human, can be negated to create an illusion of self-sufficiency and omnipotence (Bromberg, 1983). Where there have been traumatic failures in empathy the person will hold within their core self intolerable, unmanageable, raw sensory elements that can be projected into the relationship through complementary transference (Racker, 1968) and counter-transference. Benjamin (2004) describes this as a dyad that can accommodate only one mind, where the complementarity is made up of two parts of a whole in a dance of 'doer and done to' (p. 9), in which there is no space for negotiation of meaning and both parties are in opposition.

Use of relationship in the therapeutic process

In the initial stages of therapy the therapist will inevitably be invited by the client into a responsive role (Sandler, 1979) that fulfils an archaic relational template. As such the relationship becomes a source of information about the client's history and how they manage being them in relation to the other. What forms an important part of therapy is making sense of what is constellated in the relationship, unearthing and metabolising unconscious material that surfaces as each person takes the risk to feel what has been avoided, or not validated, connecting as 'like subjects' (Benjamin, 2004) in a mutually reciprocal relationship.

Atwood and Stolorow point out the significance of the interpersonal as the 'empirical domain of psychoanalytic inquiry' (1984, p. 64). However, in order to facilitate this the therapist must have an idea of their own relational templates and what in them would draw them into transference relationships. Gerson (2008) recognised an unconscious pull within the psychoanalytic profession to interpret subjective experience purely as individual phenomena. What this suggests is an inherent and unconscious defence against what Stolorow and Atwood termed 'the unbearable embeddedness of being' (1992, p. 22).

Relational supervision

Just as the eye cannot see itself without the use of a mirror I believe that we cannot know how much of ourselves we avoid in the therapeutic relationship without supervision. Whilst supervision often recognises that the therapist's counter-transference, or how they are touched by the client, is their primary tool in the process of helping the client discover themselves in the relational sphere, we are also concerned with the discovery of the bi-directionality of the relational unconscious. Below I discuss how an exploration of the myth of Echo and Narcissus illustrates the complementarity in which I found myself in the supervision group, which was then reflected in my client work. I explore how this relational organisation functions both to inoculate against destructive, primitive and unconscious experiences and to communicate them.

The story of Echo and Narcissus

There are many versions of the myth that tells the story of Echo, a woodland nymph, falling in love with Narcissus. In one version Greene and Sharman-Burke describe Hera's anger with Echo because she would not stop talking. As a punishment Hera took away Echo's power of speech so that she could only repeat the last few words of another person's voice. Meanwhile, the mother of Narcissus, anxious to protect her son, followed the guidance of the blind prophet who said that he would live into old age 'as long as he does not know himself' (ibid., 2000, p. 125). She made sure that he never saw his own reflection, and Narcissus could only surmise his image through the reactions of others.

As Narcissus went walking in the woods one day Echo fell in love with this beautiful creature and endeavoured to attract his attention. With no facility to make her presence known, she could only repeat the last word spoken. Narcissus, believing he was too beautiful for someone flawed and imperfect, cruelly dismissed her. With shame and impotent rage Echo appealed to the Gods that Narcissus know what it is like to be rejected. Her prayer was answered, and at that moment Narcissus, gazing into a woodland pool, fell in love with the beautiful image reflected on the water. He could not pull himself away, but each time he reached out to this perfect image it shimmered and shattered into a million pieces. There he perished. Echo faded away with grief and regret, so that all that was left was her voice.

Using the myth to explore my self

The myth reveals failures in self to self-object relations. Firstly, Narcissus' mother was fearful of her son's fate, and we see he failed to internalise a sense of himself. Instead he became perpetually dependent on the gaze of others. Hera was 'exasperated' with Echo's chatter, suggesting, regardless of any effort, that there was a mutual non-recognition, emptiness and meaninglessness. Her curse simply reversed the complementary roles. Echo had been effectively stripped of her authority and presence, and only noticed for how she reflected the other.

As referred to above, therapists are more likely to have experienced insufficient validation and containment, and I am no exception. In my earlier life I played the Echo role, unaware that the relationship was a result of insufficient validating and holding within the family. I bolstered my self through idealising and twinning with the other. My sense of self came from being needed, and I remained invisible. My therapy training helped me identify the conditions of worth I had assumed in relationships, and with growing knowledge of theory and experimenting within professional and personal relationships I gained an understanding and valuing of myself, and was on the road to 'know myself'.

Finding Echo in the group

The group had been running for over ten years when I joined. Members had had a long-standing experience of being in an established group with an implicit understanding of themselves in the group and an anticipation of how things were done, constituting a cultural third (Gerson, 2009), or set of unconscious assumptions. As I joined the group I experienced members as warm, and felt they were curious to know me.

On the second meeting the supervisor, after some hesitation, confessed that she couldn't recall my name, and that this had happened earlier in that day too. Another member said she had had the same experience. They presented this with curiosity, and wondered what I made of this. I was aware of two sensations: of feeling held and attended to, and simultaneously of feeling worthless and rejected.

The supervisor's choice to express her counter-transference, voicing what had presented itself within our relationship, the inter-subjective field (Ogden, 1994), touched me, and I felt the impact in both a pleasant and an unpleasant way. In response to the supervisor's comments, one member reflected on the silent, abandoned and alienated part of her self that knew what it meant to be invisible. This discussion did not trigger any meaning for me, as it had with the other group member. I remember sitting with both curiosity and emotional detachment like a protection, and as I did so I recognised this was a defence against what was constellated in the supervision group in that moment and named by my colleague that reflected a part of me.

Through the group, the supervisor's use of her counter-transference, reflection and writing about it I could glimpse contents of my unvalidated unconscious (Stolorow and Atwood, 1989), the unformed part of me, tentative in meeting the gaze of the other when there is no agenda and simply genuine curiosity. Within the intersubjective space of the group, I experienced a lack or absence for which there were no words. I was unable to assimilate what was held in the group, and instead acted from my adapted self that effectively masked over and kept out of mental reach both an unbearable and ordinary human experience of isolation and invisibility. What I noticed was the balance between the part of me that was acting from my adapted self, the self that 'complements' the other, Echo, and the real self that acts from an autonomous, spontaneous core.

What light does this throw on what, by unconscious default, I was offering to clients within the therapeutic relationship? I realised a personal and unconscious pull to set myself up as a self-object, and how I endeavoured to be someone who behaves perfectly, as if I were Echo, not present, without any sense of my own voice or authority. Alongside this I was of course conscious that my role was to remain connected and attuned to the client in the inevitable and manageable disappointments in meeting their needs. As Winnicott pointed out, an 'object that behaves perfectly becomes no better than a hallucination' (1953, p. 11), and this reminds me of how Echo diminished in substance and faded away.

Finding myself in the group

I will describe an encounter in the supervision group and my interpretation of it that revealed how I unconsciously treated my self as a separate self, and not an ever-changing entity that forms and shifts within the self-other relational system.

On the third meeting I was due to present a paper for discussion in the educational section of our meeting. I didn't get very far before one group member asked me a question. I went blank. Although the supervisor stepped in with prompts and encouragement I did not find my words or any thoughts. The supervisor noticed that she felt as if she too had lost her mind. I continued with my presentation but quite quickly opened it up for group discussion. The supervisor wondered if she remained the facilitator during the education slot of the supervision or if the presenter was the facilitator. Group members engaged in the topic and said they had found it interesting. Consciously, I was disappointed, feeling that I had failed to live up to my own expectations. I felt humiliation that I could not hold the session on my own, and that the supervisor had stepped in to help me.

The illusion of self containment

Later, at home, I fell into a shame reaction. I felt caught in my own thoughts and feelings and felt this deep, dark weight in my stomach like a growing black hole that was going to consume me. I felt a failure and stupid and how everyone in the group would think really badly of me. I connected with my mind and thoughts that were nurturing and reasonable. Although this disarmed the invading visceral attack I needed to make sense of it.

I took *my* experience to my therapist and recognised the grief I felt in the reality of being vulnerable and dependent when needing help, hating being imperfect, hating not knowing or being able to manage everything. This part of me wanted to be omnipotent and invulnerable. In this process I could glimpse the dissociated, unprocessed element of anger that sat right beside fear of abandonment and being nothing. What I did not know then was that I interpreted my primitive feelings exclusively as an indicator of my pathology, as if I was a 'self contained individual who can generate his or her own knowledge and is solely responsible for his own fate' (Gerson, 2008).

I found a reflection of myself in Narcissus when I could not tolerate the misunderstanding and non-recognition I saw in the faces of the group members. I needed them to mirror back to me a positive image, to be an Echo for me. I recognised the group had evoked a strong self-object transference dynamic that I am sure was linked to my rating the members and the supervisor highly and wanting to be accepted, and at the same time fearing I could not live up to this ideal. Caught in an unconscious idealising transference I was dependent on the other reflecting back to me my worth and authority, validating me and yet experienced myself as a bounded and autonomous self.

I did not at this point feel able to take my feelings into the group.

Myself in relationship

When the supervisor asked the question of whether she remained the facilitator during the educational section I believe she was attempting to make sense of the enactment that felt fuelled by primitive dependency. In this instance my dependency needs had been evoked but the supervisor, naming her subjectivity, became curious about dependency in the group and our need of her. I feel she attended to the question of who held the space if unconscious processes surfaced, recognising that groups and relationships are powerful provocateurs of unconscious needs, regardless of the conscious agenda. In subsequent sessions a number of group members explored their core experience of being in the group and I could normalise my personal feelings and recognise them as responses to daring to 'be' and belong as an authentic, potent and creative self. For all the time the group had not collectively processed unbearable and unconscious elements that belonged to the group, such as entitlement, dependency needs to belong or feel validated, we explored defensive manoeuvres that led to separateness or merger. I noticed feeling ambivalent, minimising the importance of the group, judging members of the group (in my head) and the group itself, and got busy thinking about group theory with the hope of working it out intellectually! I recognise these manoeuvres as attempts to maintain my primitive defence to be omnipotent, invulnerable and invisible.

Within my shame reaction I had discovered an alien fantasy that the supervisor was envious of me. In time I transferentially recognised my sister in the supervisor whom I idealised, and who envied me for taking valuable attention away from her when I was born and fiercely protected the position of the one who could be and do better than me. It felt much harder to realise the envy that I felt. In the process of discovering my primitive envy I had discovered an archaic relational template personified by Echo with Narcissus that I had hitherto been unaware of. I realise how this relational template played out in the group as I found the primitive part of me that raged at how the supervisor dared so easily take up her space and authority and use her voice so eloquently? Daring to stay in relationship to the group enabled me to find and make sense of an important element within my unconscious.

I understand now that to be 'free to act' (Symington, 1983) and free to speak within a containing relationship I need acceptance of my primitive wishes and affects. I realise that I behaved as if I was psychologically separate or complementary through my unconscious fear of my primitive destructive psyche. Mollon comments that 'It is this presymbolic dimension which is the *ultimate* source of dread, terror and paranoia – indeed the source of ubiquitous impulses to abuse and terrorize one's fellow human beings' (2001, p. 10). The myth of Echo and Narcissus brings to light the sadistic and masochistic potential in complementarity where projective identification is the means by which relief from the unbearable or unknowable is sought.

The supervision group enabled my discovery because the supervisor failed to fulfil the idealised role alongside bringing her authority and entitlement to bear in the service of the group. She rejected the invitation to be Narcissus and yet articulated her understanding of the idealising transference in the group. It was in exploring the role of supervision with a client that the group helped me to understand that I can be both related and separate to recognise that my experience was important information that belonged to the relationship.

The group as a supervision group

The remit of the relational supervision group is to create a relational space for each member to bring clients. I see the boundary of the group extending to include the clients that are brought incorporating their known and unknown story. Inevitably what will be brought to the group are intolerable elements (Bion, 1962), such as loss and trauma, that are fragmented, chaotic and split off alongside unformed aspects of self that have not come to life within an unvalidating environment (Stolorow and Atwood, 1989).

Clinical example: Chris

Chris had an older sister and parents with few aspirations to learn about the world, travel or strive in careers. In spite of this he remembered his father pushing him to be the best at school and not validating any achievements. He remembered his mother's expression 'self praise is no recommendation'. He did not feel as if he had been taken seriously. He was a day-dreamer, having grandiose fantasies about becoming a famous author, businessman or (in his younger days) rock star. Chris had left home but drifted through much of his life, opting out, under-achieving. He was frustrated with himself for being passive and not finishing things, and did not see himself as someone who could succeed. He discounted his achievements, including attaining a degree as a mature student, gaining professional qualifications and work in a prestigious company. He described himself as confident in social situations but as the joker, and was accommodating, gently spoken and quiet. He hated people who had a strong sense of entitlement or who were forceful in getting what they wanted. There was anger buttoned up inside a calm, accommodating persona. He had come to therapy on securing a new job, hoping to address his lack of confidence.

The therapy and our relationship

Chris brought the vulnerability of an unformed or unvalidated self constituted by what he believed he was supposed to be. At the same time he longed for freedom to be himself, whatever that was. I felt that I was needed, and was being used, as a self-object within an idealising and mirroring transference.

The therapy was psycho-educational at first, thinking together about what he needed to feel confident. In time he developed an ability to think about his feelings and his needs, almost filling himself in like a picture in a colouring book. I believed we had created a relationship where we could play, using sandtray, dreams, stories and roleplay through which Chris could articulate some of his internal world, discovering his needs and vulnerabilities, particularly his fear and shame. I felt that we were on the road by which 'he would know himself' (see p. 80), redressing Narcissus' original wound.

On several occasions he brought his dreams, and one in particular seemed to illustrate our relationship. He described driving a car around a circular racing track with a person at the centre holding a clipboard. He felt confident going round and round but was aware of another track that was slightly hidden with some obstacles in the way. He was aware of not wanting to go there. On waking he had immediately equated this dream to us, him in the car and me as the coach. He was really pleased that he had mastered the driving, being someone who had failed his driving test nine times and was not interested in cars. It felt symbolic of him mastering his world. He was very aware that he was not ready and did not want to leave the track for this other one.

What I struggled with

Invariably at the start of sessions I would ask him how he was and he would say 'normal'. He brought a passivity, with no image of himself, seeing me as the expert. I often checked out with him what he needed, inviting him to take the initiative, whereupon he would look flustered and say that he wanted more of the same, what I was doing was working, he was gaining all the time in confidence, learning how to assert himself and finding his creativity, so he wanted more of it. His need felt like an expectancy, and I noticed being less spontaneous and more in my head. There was a part of me that felt responsible for him. I decided to take him to the supervision group to explore my growing sense that we had fallen into a chronic enactment or complementarity.

Taking Chris to the group

I described Chris, our work together and my feelings, and then I stepped into the 'Balint Chair' to observe the group. The group were quiet and still as they settled and noticed how my presentation had impacted them. After a silence someone spoke: 'I've got an image of a soft, squashy sponge.' Silence followed and then another person punctured the stillness: 'I can't help wondering what they do. She's been seeing him for *three years*. What do they do together?' I noticed thinking that the comment felt harsh and braced myself for criticism. I noticed another person frowning in what felt like a rising energy in the group, and she declared, 'I can't take him seriously.' Another person interjected with what felt like disgust: 'Does he want his mother?', with the former person following on, 'I want him to *do* something.' A further person spoke: 'Where is Gina's authority?' The irritation and impatience was palpable.

One member described an image she had of Chris and me in the belly of a whale and a deadness and frustration crept into the group, as if the whale had dived down into the depths of the ocean, out of reach. The same person puzzled, as if trying to find something out of sight, and said 'it feels like an aggression in Gina's kindness. It feels like she is hiding something.' I was surprised and didn't relate to what she was saying.

The group discussed the relationship between Chris and me as if still inside the whale, looking for the way out. They thought if I acted he would become passive. They wondered if he diminished himself for fear, of coming alive and losing me. Then someone punctuated the discussion with the comment, 'It's like: "keep dead and stay related"', uttered like a curse. The group fell quiet.

The supervisor then relayed her thoughts, which took up another side of the polarity. 'I'm noticing what interests me about Chris. Come on, here is someone who is writing stories and a film script. I would be really interested to know what he writes about. He is planning to live in another country, the other side of the world. That really takes some doing.' I noticed myself breathe more freely.

I was invited back into the group to discuss my thoughts. I said that I had heard the different feelings, particularly impatience, and I said that I found this useful to help me think about what I did feel when I was with him. I said that I heard their frustration at not being able to find Chris or me and how I needed to think about owning my own authority. I felt they had given me brutally honest feedback in a caring way.

The supervisor rounded off our discussion by saying,

> I think that Chris has no sense of entitlement, and has not discovered that about himself yet. There certainly have been opposing reactions from the group from deadness and disconnection to anger and I wonder if your job, Gina, is to stay alive and keep connected with yourself. I think that he has come a long way and done good things.

Reflecting on the process

I understood that each member of the group used their own subjectivity both to generate, and be influenced by, the 'intersubjective analytic third' (Ogden, 1994). What this created was a representation, rather like a staged play, of

Chris' and my relationship. Each member was an actor in the play (Cassorla, 2005), and from their participation, informed by their own life experience, they could use their feelings to bring the play to life. I was sure that Chris' father, mother and sister came onto the stage.

I understand that the group were struggling to get a sense of Chris and me. Through their discussion they represented the merging in the relationship and articulated it through images of a soft, squashy sponge and the whale. I could see the surge of irritation and frustration, and then the thinking that seemed intent on breaking or transforming this subjugating, negative third (Ogden, 1994), 'where there is an erasure of the in-between – an inverse mirror relation, a complementary dyad concealing an unconscious symmetry' (Benjamin, 2004, p. 10). It felt as if the group were struggling to be a 'symbolic' or 'analytic' third (Lacan, 1977) between Chris and me to find both of us. I witnessed the deadening effect it had in the group. What I realised from the group was how I had got pulled into becoming the ever more perfect reflector for Chris. What I appeared to be was a loving 'mother', and how I felt was an unreal, 'going through the motions mother' in a perfectly 'normal' relationship that plastered over an absence (Green, 1986).

Observing the group members' feelings I could see the importance of my subjectivity and glimpsed what existed in the therapy relationship that had not been named, much like Echo's mute rage and Hera's exasperation. Bollas writes that 'in order to find the patient we must look for him in ourselves' (1987, p. 202). I needed to feel what was being split off and begin to articulate my experience in order to help Chris begin to find another way to process this unknowable core.

Similarly to my process in the group, described earlier, where the group had helped me to metabolise my envy, I was being called to provide the same function for Chris. Just as I had done in the group I saw that Chris was managing these deeper feelings of shame, fear and failure through self-blame and self-loathing. Although dependent on me in the self-object transference, I believe he experienced himself as self-contained.

I needed to value my experience and hold my narcissistically wounded self that mirrored that self in Chris. This meant being real and sharing my 'exasperation'. In order to do this I needed to hold the tension between identificatory oneness and the observing function (Benjamin, 2004).

The supervisor and group members were modelling this use of self particularly in finding what in Chris they could relate to and enjoy, and maintaining a freedom to feel and say what they liked. I believed this was helpful in restoring vitality into the relationship.

How I used my learning from supervision

The group had helped me find my potency. I felt more able to stay alive in the relationship, to challenge Chris by acknowledging his worth in our relationship. I referred to his dream and wondered what it would feel like if I was to sit in the car next to him. He looked puzzled and frightened. He said little and failed to turn up to the next session, later saying that he had forgotten. I reflected on what his absence might mean, recalling how challenged I felt in the group to be seen. I was no longer being 'killed off by kindness', and I reflected that he probably found this quite shocking. I decided not to focus on his absence, for in the subsequent sessions Chris brought himself into the relationship. A space had opened between us where he felt able to talk about feelings of shame at being seen. I think he was tentatively stepping into the relationship not as Echo or Narcissus but as a real and imperfect being.

These moments of meeting were fleeting and new for Chris. In essence the supervision had revived me, enabled me to be more conscious and become more real (Winnicott, 1968), and together we began to face the existential reality of what it meant to be in relationship.

In the remaining sessions before Chris left to go travelling he expressed his wish that we could continue, and wondered if he might find a therapist like me in Australia. I challenged him to accept that we were ending, at least for now. He responded with a flash of anger and shame. This important moment got lost as we managed as much as we could do to be who we were at that point in time.

I had not yet fully identified the pull in me to be Echo, a very effective mirror as in a one-person psychology. At this point with Chris I was not fully able to use the relationship as a container for the wrath, exasperation, worthlessness and dependency needs that were evoked in the relationship between Chris and me. Although the supervision experience hardly made waves in this therapeutic relationship, with time and with writing this chapter I have changed profoundly and hold the potential, if Chris did return, thinking of his dream, to help him drive on the track of life that he chooses, interdependent and individuated.

Clinical implications of learning about, and using, my self

To work at depth and relationally it is fundamentally important to be available, to be able to use one's human experience and to own one's vulnerability. I have a much fuller understanding of my own vulnerabilities through the experience in the supervision group and my subsequent discoveries in therapy.

Exploring the meanings inherent for me in the myth of Narcissus and Echo has been painful at a personal level but has also revealed to me the clinical implications of the personal. By coming alive in my self I became more conscious of the role Chris had recruited me to take; a role which was compatible with my Echo adaptation. I now understand that the intersubjective space between therapist and client will necessarily be unprocessed and unknown, for we will bring ourselves into relationship in the only way we know how. It seems clear to me now that it is necessary for a therapist to be pulled out of shape in an attempt to attune to their client, that in doing so valuable information will be revealed about the client's inner world. Additionally, the therapist must consider how role-responsiveness may play into their self-other object relations, blinding them to information or experience that is essential to the client.

Transforming Narcissus and Echo

I was able to find the Echo in me with some empathy for that self, who was not able to address Narcissus (my projection onto the group and clients) because of her dependence on him and her longing that he would validate her. Learning to be me meant I could puncture Narcissus' bubble, that it would potentially liberate him to experience himself and learn the reality of himself as unavoidably related to others and an imperfect being. In my reading around this subject I found a most valuable theoretical underpinning to support my newly awakened conscious in Benjamin, who describes so wonderfully well how much we are denying in the client when we avoid 'bumping into their bruises or jabbing them while stitching them up' (2004, p. 11). I now fully understood how I blocked my potency for fear of inflicting a traumatising wound, and did not recognise the holding potential firmly located within the intersubjective space between us.

Complementarity in the group

This refers to a type of stuck-ness of roles in relatedness (see reference to Benjamin above). In the group, for example, the supervisor or group members may unknowingly be fulfilling archaic self-object transferences where there is an unconscious striving towards positive validation, which can easily mask a lack of self-worth or authority.

The supervisor pulled me out of this role by engaging with me out of role, by 'forgetting my name'. This was the pull towards a transformative engagement, from daring to experience and pay attention to, no matter how crazy or scary, the phenomena that present within the intersubjective relationship. The deep attunement in the group, alongside an intuitive spontaneity, often evoking difficult feelings in the other, as well as potential conflict, enabled important insight about the unconscious realm.

Conclusion

This chapter has been an account of my journey in the supervision group and how it has been a part of my personal development in the service of the client. I have explored how a relationship can become a complementarity characterised by Narcissus at the woodland pool unable to live, stuck in time, dependent on an illusory other, unable to break away but unfulfilled, longing, striving.

The payoff of narcissism within our culture (Lasch, 1977; May, 1991; Gerhardt, 2010) is the avoidance of our existential reality of uncertainty, of not being in control, of loss, of our humanness. As therapists we cannot be entirely immune to this wish and the struggle to keep unconscious what has previously been split off. We can only strive to be open to notice how clues materialise in our own minds and in our relationships.

The relational supervision group has provided a container, or a map, for me as a therapist and as a person who has grappled with what it means to be me in relationship, particularly within the supervision group and with my clients. My struggle to bring my core self into relationship continues and facilitates my development and growth and forms the essence of my authority. Paradoxically, it is through acceptance of my embeddedness within the matrix of relationships that I find myself. When I feel ashamed, impotent, alone, envious, angry and hateful I can use my experience to attune to and be separate from my clients and what they bring.

The image I hold that describes my supervision process is being taken by the hand by those in my therapeutic community leading me into the woodland pool. I step down into the water and see around me other swimmers including Echo and Narcissus. The water is dark and I cannot see much below the surface. I use every sense in me to test out if the water will hold me and gradually, gradually move my body to find that I can swim.

Chapter 6

Through the glass darkly

How Alice finds herself in the eye of the tempest's storm, and emerges into a place of mirrored reflection

Jane Todd

In this chapter I describe my experiences in the relational supervision group when I explored how a potential rupture with a client threatened the frame of our therapeutic relationship. I analyse how my use of the supervision group facilitated an intersubjective re-connection with self and client and a non-regressive response to the rupture. I integrate a relational theoretical perspective throughout the chapter.

Reciprocity and recognition

I have been a member of my supervision group for ten years. The culture of the supervision group is embedded firmly in the collaborative aspect of supervision (Carroll and Tholstrup, 2001), namely intersubjectivity. The group offers a creative space in which the intersubjective process allows for an innovative discussion, in which we consider the impact of therapist to client, client to therapist alongside group to member, member to group, member to supervisor. There is both a mutuality (in many varieties, including recognition, influence or empathy) and a respect for what is both individual and what is shared. There is a culture, evolved over the years of working together of encouragement for both professional growth and personal authority, that we can all feel that 'I am the doer who does, I am the author of my acts, by being with another ... who recognises her acts, her feelings, her intentions, her independence' (Benjamin, 1988, p. 21). It is the knowing of self through other subjects whilst appreciating the uniqueness of each individual that offers the perspective 'that the other whom the self meets is also a self, a subject in his or her own right' (Benjamin, 1988, p. 20).

Whilst this is not a therapy group, members are encouraged to participate fully in elaborating and exploring all self-structures – primitive or otherwise. It is acknowledged that regression will be an inevitable part of the supervision process – whether as a counter-transferential response or as a result of our own self-representations – but it is understood as offering potentially trans-formational information for both self and clients. For example, working with such contemplative creativity enables clues to emerge in order to examine transference/counter-transference reactions, dreams, metaphors and interpret-ations which offer us what was previously unknown or unspeakable for both client and self.

The diamond in the group's structure comes from the sharing of minds, the finding of one's own mind/self agency through mutual recognition: of seeing and being seen. This allows the unconscious to emerge, revealing our self-representations alongside the other as separate but inter-related beings. The intra-psychic and intersubjective processes are equally import-ant, for without the intra-psychic aspect, the interpersonal becomes one-dimensional.

Identity and language

It is the juxtaposition of the individual within the group that mirrors the per-sonal and professional process. What has been a commonality within the group is a shared experience and a shared language. Within the intersubjective domain, language also offers a way of relating to the other: Stern's (1985) work reminds us about 'mutually negotiated meanings' that facilitate growth and development. This is something that has also been used to address emer-ging themes in the group, as a way of discussing and co-creatively identi-fying the internalised worlds of self, client and group. What is important is the *meaning-making*: of what is both shared and individual. We all have our own wounds, our own relational patterns, which are both personal and uni-versal. The central themes of human existence and primitive feelings such as envy, fear, hate and destruction, emerge within the group process and what then becomes most crucial is the meaning-making of these varied experiences within the context in which they arrive.

I will now describe my client and our therapeutic relationship as presented to my supervision group.

Clinical example

Background

Marisa is an Anglo-Asian woman in her mid forties, married with three chil-dren. She came into therapy with issues around attachment and a persistent feeling of emptiness which was repeatedly acted out in both her personal and professional life. She presented with difficulty in tolerating frustration, small capacity for trust and a permanent feeling of emptiness. She had a fear of engulfment and used distancing defences to protect herself.

History

Marisa is the oldest child of an emotionally absent mother and an alcoholic, gambling businessman father, both from working-class backgrounds. She has three siblings. From a young age, they were regularly abused physically by their father, and this lasted until her mid-teens. Her mother knew about it yet did nothing to protect them. Marisa believed the only way to survive was to study hard at school and get out as soon as she could. She has no contact with her father now and limited contact with her mother. She has been very successful in building up her own company and establishing a stable home life with her husband and children.

She reported that at times she did not want to be in any relationships, acknowledging that when she gets scared of too much intimacy she knows that her script issue is to withdraw physically or dissociate; I knew that at some point this would occur in our relationship. Davies and Frawley's work on dissociation reminds us of how clients manage their trauma, separating it as a disconnected part of themselves and how the therapist must be mindful of the fact that they are 'undertaking the treatment of two people; an adult who struggles to succeed, relate, gain acceptance … and a child who… strives to remember and find a voice with which to scream her outrage at the world' (1994, p. 67). She reported regularly walking around her house in a daze feeling numb, which is reflected in the work of Rothschild (2000) and DeYoung (2003), who examine the trance states that survivors of trauma use in order to prevent painful memories from being conscious. I knew Marisa was telling me something about her internal world for which she had no words yet. Marisa's mistrust of the other meant that it took some time to establish a working alliance between us. Masterson states that 'the patient will resist allying his emotions with the therapist because it means giving up his usual method of avoiding painful feelings of separation anxiety and abandonment depression' (1988, p. 132).

Our work focused at this time on her story of her childhood, the history of her relationships, themes of abandonment and engulfment and what was emerging within our intersubjective field. Marisa could be extremely amusing: she would act out stories using characters and voices and I found myself simultaneously amused and bemused. It was as if she had a dressing-up box, and I wondered what was lying hidden beneath the silk scarves and bejewelled costumes. I knew there was something that felt beyond my reach, both unknown and unspoken.

Transference acting out

The first signs of our therapeutic rupture occurred when Marisa began a new post as a counsellor, which introduced her to a new supervisor. She began to have strong counter-transferential feelings towards him as the supervision progressed, which manifested in her forgetting the time of her supervision with him, getting lost on the way, falling over when she went there. She said it was like beginning to go mad and living in *Alice in Wonderland*, and it began to feel to both of us that she was 'losing her mind' in some way. Marisa reported feeling that she was on the outside looking in, like Alice through the looking glass. The themes of appearance, self-regard and trying to make sense of things absurd certainly echoed this story. Kilborn's *Disappearing Persons* (2002) examines the tale's themes of identity and confusion through its use of archetypal images and the paradox of feeling conspicuous whilst being unable to imagine oneself through the eyes of another. How was Marisa seeing herself through me?

Stuthridge writes that 'During an enactment, fault lines within the self erupt in the therapy relationship' (2012, p. 245) and things certainly began to get rocky as the inevitable fault lines appeared. Marisa began to idealise me, whilst simultaneously attacking herself, saying 'You seem so serene' and 'I don't fit in this therapy world and everyone else does.' Hargaden and Sills remind us of the idealising transference as a desire to locate the 'strength and calm' in the other as a way of addressing early ruptures (2002, p. 151). Davies and Frawley refer to: 'The analyst tries to steer a course through the storm, knowing that all involved will be tossed around unmercifully and that there will be periods when all sense of direction and purpose will be lost' (1994, p. 85) I thought of the developmental level at which Marisa was functioning. I knew she was employing a splitting defence in order to achieve a form of object constancy with me, as in when the child hates the mother and thus wants to annihilate her, yet at the same time needs to see her as still existing and there for the child once the feelings have subsided (Johnson, 1994).

Our work became focused on a tiny pinhead, namely the supervisory relationship and Marisa's splitting reactions to him as she moved between seeing him as a shining star in the firmament and a forbidden planet. He may as well have been in the room with us. I envisaged the supervisor as a wolf, knocking at my very door, a re-enactment of Marisa's experience of her father's ruthlessness and betrayal. How did Marisa see him? Traumatised clients often feel others have supernatural powers (DeYoung 2003), and Marisa repeatedly referred to the supervisor as a magician. I considered the archetype of the trickster in Alice, as manifested by several characters, such as the Mad Hatter, as we examined the meaning-making of what was happening, both inside the room and outside in the context of her script. Marisa's experience of feeling lost echoed Alice's struggle of not being able to recognise herself through the Wonderland creatures and vice versa. I could almost see her following the White Rabbit only to find that 'There were doors all round the hall, but they were all locked ... she walked sadly down the middle, wondering how she was ever to get out again' (Carroll, 1865, p. 15).

As the therapy progressed I began to feel my self shrinking like a telescope, rather like Alice when she had drunk from the bottle marked 'Poison'. I thought about the context of my own personal experiences of family. My family came from the same part of England, with a similar language. I wondered about experiences we shared, in particular how our families responded to emotional scenarios and the impact that had made. I came from a family where education and hard work were seen as an essential way of being, and what was seen as emotionally difficult was pushed under the carpet. My coping mechanism was to say nothing, watch in a hyper-vigilant way whilst feeling small and disconnected, yearning for something I could not describe. The silence was deafening. I would crave both actions and connections and sought them out through books or my imagination. Instinctively, I knew that we shared a need to be recognised by the other, for them to reach out. My understanding of the enactment transference/counter-transference dynamics was reflected in Gabbard and Wilkinson's thoughts that 'the deadness or emptiness experienced by the patient may foster complementary feelings of helplessness ... in the psychotherapist' (1994, p. 60). But who was helpless? The roles felt persistently interchangeable between us; it felt like we had been reduced to binary oppositions: 'either I am guilty or I am victim, either you really let me down or I expect too much, either you are the best therapist in the whole world or you suck' (Aron, 2013, p. 398). Marisa's transference shifted as the supervisor became idealised, and I began to fall from grace in Marisa's eyes, feeling the ever-increasing onslaught of therapeutic arrows coming my way.

Enactment

Three months later, Marisa came to a session in a state of considerable distress. She reported that the supervisor told her that she needed to come into therapy with him in order to look at her strong counter-transferential response to him. She said she felt powerless against him and had agreed to do this but was afraid I was going to be upset or angry with her for leaving. She declared that 'If I were you, I wouldn't work with me.' I was curious about Marisa's apparent increasing alliance with the supervisor. Where was her mind and why was she so apparently compliant to his wishes? It was as if she had reduced herself and our therapeutic relationship to the point of annihilation. Eigen's writings on the annihilated self reflect some of the paradoxical themes in *Alice in Wonderland*, namely those of 'seeing what shouldn't be seen' and 'we are drawn to what blinds us' (2006a, p. 27). What was Marisa being drawn into in this re-enactment? Johnson's work on our fearful reactions to the threat of annihilation-abandonment and our various defensive tactics underlines the paradoxical 'healing crisis, which may be either resisted or worked through' (1994, p. 176). I wondered about the link between her apparent powerlessness as aspects of herself that craved recognition whilst feeling undeserving of being seen. I knew Marisa's representations of her caregivers were conflicted and split, and through her words I heard the possible identification with her abusive father: 'Sometimes the child … excuses or rationalises the failure of protection by attributing it to her own unworthiness. More commonly, the child idealises the abusive parent and displaces all her rage onto the non-offending parent' (Herman, 1992, p. 106).

At this stage, my feelings oscillated between rage with the supervisor, feeling 'How dare you do this to her/us/me?' combined with 'What is the point? He will be more powerful than me.' It felt agonising and paralysing. I could see the rage/despair as positions of complementarity – I felt stuck, cast in a seemingly paralysing spell, that something was being done to me. 'Because the transference communicated through projective identification is so intense and so alien to the therapist, the clinician's reactions frequently include disorganisation of her thinking capacities' (Davies and Frawley, 1994, p. 161). I was aware that I was feeling a toxic mix of masochistic helplessness alongside aggression towards Marisa's supervisor. So what was this telling me about Marisa? Maybe this was how Marisa had felt as a child and was experiencing now in this re-enactment. Was Marisa projecting the very powerful un-expressed rage she felt as a child? In bringing my focus on Marisa's internal world (rather than the external feelings of sadism towards the supervisor) I felt there were clues in the masochism in this narrative: How did it reflect Marisa's self structures? I thought about both Marisa and I feeling alone within this story, even though we were together: 'The masochist despairs of ever holding the attention or winning the recognition of the other, of being securely held in the others' mind … Masochism can be seen … as a strategy for escaping aloneness, but also as a search for aloneness *with* the other' (Benjamin, 1988, p. 72). This highlighted the motif of Alice's story: the confusion arising from an identity crisis and the desire to be found. Ahh! Marisa had found a very powerful way of letting me know she needed both recognition and contact. She certainly had my attention.

Maroda states that: 'Without a regressive phase in treatment, no matter how many sessions a week … all that results is a supportive environment.' (2004, p. 72). What had happened needed to happen. Little (2012, p. 110) underscores this: 'An enactment may be usefully considered to be part of a larger sequence of events during therapy … The therapeutic significance of the enactment lies in *how it is dealt with*, not in the enactment itself' (p. 110, italics mine).

As I wrestled with how to respond and to contain my own experiences I realised I needed to use my own internalised container in order to have a response that both of us could bear. I knew what to aim for: 'successful handling of the therapist's countertransferential participation in the patient's transferential enactments is a matter of balance' (Stark, 1999, p. 118). I knew that if I became unbalanced my counter-transference could take me away from the optimal position of Stark's 'semipermeability' – that is being willing to absorb the client's impact but not be totally subsumed by it. I felt I was moving backwards and forwards between observer and participant, and was definitely in a place of 'unwitting enactment'. Little's work on optimal neutrality refers to 'a state of mind, a non-judgmental stance … attempts to find a balance between engagement and observation as well as balancing an attitude … and involves acceptance of all parts of the client' (2012, p. 112). Marisa had engaged me in experiencing many feelings as a way of drawing me as an object into her own subjective, internal experiences and what felt elusive was the optimal balance between being in a neutral, reflective space and using myself to understand Marisa's relational dynamics.

Contemplative creativity

Alice's 'curiouser and curiouser' phrase came to mind as I examined my counter-transference. Initially I reconnected with an intuitive trust in my own creative abilities in order to understand and ultimately to find what Marisa needed me to see. I thought of her story of horrific abuse and the unspeakable aspects of that experience for Marisa and as I sat with the wordlessness of her narrative, I imagined that we had both tumbled down a hole, just like Alice did, and had emerged into a stormy sea. Putting on my imaginary life-jacket,

I wondered about Alice fearing she would literally drown in her own tears she had cried when she was nine feet high, as I saw Marisa sleep-walking between the waves. When it came to repairing this rupture, I felt that if I did not find a way of reaching her, Marisa could remain unfound, resulting in the ultimate betrayal: therapeutic abandonment.

Taking Marisa to relational supervision

In this section, I will illustrate how I used the relational supervision group to recognise, work through and transform the re-enactment and potential rupture I was struggling with in my work with Marisa.

I presented my client to the group, giving a brief history and describing the present circumstances within our relationship. I was then invited to take what is referred to as the Balint Chair (see Chapter 1), whilst the group processed what they had made from the presentation, including thoughts, feelings, metaphors and any other associations that arose. The presenting supervisee is referred to in the third person and not addressed directly in this process, which can sometimes take as long as an hour. This creates a receptive, analytic space in which the supervisee can *enter into* the client's internal world and object relations. These interpretations are verbalised by the group members while the supervisor is both an authentic participant and through reflection and understanding offers containment and assimilation for the group and presenting supervisee.

Group process

The following is an edited version of the process, followed by theoretical perspectives and personal reflections. It takes into account the robustness of all participants of the group.

JANE: So, guys ... that's the story of me and my client. I can't believe how livid I feel! It feels like there is a wolf at the door of my therapy room, huffing and puffing and trying to get in. Well, my house is not made of straw and I am not, just not letting him in. No way, no way. I feel something disastrous is going to happen.(Pause as group processes)

LIZ: At first when Jane was talking I felt so, so *angry*, and now I've got a real feeling of scare, real scare. Not sure who it belongs to yet ... so, I wonder ... does Marisa want Jane to protect her from this person, to be really strong and say 'no' to him? Then I went off into thinking about mothers and females in this story ... what do they mean to this client?

DOROTHEE: Yes, I get that too. I feel so angry towards both this client's supervisor and the client herself .... It feels like they are both trying to annihilate Jane somehow, wipe her out. And I also feel very confused ... Why, why, why does Jane's client say she wants to leave now, why is she going to him?

JOAN: Well, don't you think she is attacking Jane's boundary the way hers is or was attacked? I've gone into thinking about boundaries, protection, potency. Where is Jane's aggression? Marisa seems to be caught up in making her bad ... well, Jane's bad, mother's bad. Somehow it feels like all females are rubbish or rubbished and that this supervisor is somehow idolised in some way? ... Marisa feels like she's really showing her rage to Jane, her sadism if you like, and it feels like this has turned Jane into a helpless, masochistic version of herself?

FARI: Yes, I'm sitting here thinking this client is angry with Jane but wanting something else at the same time. If she isn't protected, she's going to return to a new version of Dad. I have an image of someone who feels very vulnerable ... no, absolutely petrified.

SUPERVISOR: There is definitely an entangling of systems here, a system of powerlessness/inadequacy. What women are invited to be or feel in this story is to somehow be inadequate under the fire of misogyny and the patriarchal system. Jane's very authority is being pulled out from under her, which is also her client's story. Her job is to hold her ground, to feel and connect with her own strength.

CATE: Yes, I've gone off on a tangent here about the fantasy aspect in this story ... the 'Rescue me' aspect ... her saying 'I wouldn't work with me' is her plea, saying '*Please* work with me ... don't leave me alone with him.' The word injustice keeps coming into my mind, and that Jane believes her the way her real mother did not. Not just believe but to act on it too! My thoughts went to what's going on between Jane and her client ... that they both feel abused here? This whole situation now is encouraging Jane into somehow being a disempowered version of who she really is. I don't know her in this story. The rug is being pulled out from under Jane, and there is nothing under the rug. I know I feel absolutely furious.

SUPERVISOR: Thank you for that, Cate. Yes, that has helped me clarify something. She needs to know Jane is not going anywhere and that she will hold her ground ... Jane needs to feel the strength going back into her ... it has been sucked out of her as she has become seduced by the story. I know she has it, but where is her therapeutic authority?

DOROTHEE: Yes, my mind keeps going over her saying she is leaving. It's as if she has left already and we are picking up the pieces. That isn't the point. She needs to stay and work this through with someone who really knows her story and to make sense of it. And I keep seeing an image of Jane and her client and that they are interchangeable, merging and separating, but I can't get hold of any shape, it keeps changing ... along the lines of containing something uncontainable.

SUPERVISOR: I am really wondering about something here. Where is Jane's mind and where is her client's? I have found my own mind wandering. We have heard the client say her supervisor says she needs to work with him. But what does *she* think about it? There is an absence of mind ... which made it hard for me to connect with this story. I kept wondering, Whose story is this? I am thinking about the client's mind and want to say 'Never mind what this supervisor says, what about *your* mind?' The work is to put it back to Marisa so she can think about it and ask *her* what she believes the therapeutic relationship is about, and what it means to her.

CATE: I think the client has been seduced by this supervisor. God, that feels horrible ... There is a part of her that is flattered by all the attention – she feels special again, or does she? Something like she thinks unconsciously, I've stirred something up in this man and either I have to keep him from acting out further *or* I have power over him *or* I feel special even if it feels awful. She needs Jane to help her make sense of this and she can't give in to him. No. No! The first thing Jane needs to be is to be a woman with a strong identity, one who is not going to give in ...

SUPERVISOR: I am now thinking of the notion of the third. That is what is missing here. It sounds like the whole process has got caught up in the content of the client being lost and using this as a third is very important. *All* of these things need to be talked about vigorously: the themes of abuse, power, danger, mother, father, etc. Thinking about Jane talking about huffing and puffing ... this client needs to find the wolf within herself. And she needs to know Jane *can* and *will* survive this, and not collapse in the face of it. So what needs to be thought about here is the third and mentalisation.

JOAN: Yes, I've got a feeling, like some of the others have said, feeling so furious with the client's supervisor ... it feels like he's trying to push through the boundary Jane has spent years co-creating with her client. It does feel that there is something sadistic/masochistic mixed up in this too. It feels sticky, nasty. And I know I'm feeling quite sadistic to all three in this story ... I half want to say 'Sort yourself out now!'

SUPERVISOR: Well, the real task here is to be her therapist and to say to her, 'I think we have gone a long way. You have brought some important things to me, such as Mother, Father, abuse, danger, protection … that is why we are here at a crossroads, and it is important that you and I make meaning of it here in this room.' Along the lines of: 'I have been thinking of you and would like to offer you my thoughts. What do you think, what is your reaction?' Ask her for her response, what she shares of her mind.

The session ended with a summing up of the process led by the supervisor. I was invited to 'come back into the group' and share my reflections on what I had felt/seen/heard as a result of the group process.

Personal reflections on the group process

As the group talked, I realised I was rapidly making notes in shorthand, which was very unusual for me; my notes looked like I had transcribed something from a court room, statements for the defence or prosecution. I knew I wanted to capture something within the language the group were speaking, rather like Alice when she asks, 'Would you tell me, please, which way I ought to go from here?' (Carroll, 1865, p. 75). The language within the book is symbolic in itself, with constant riddles, puns and the issue of meaning. So, what was my meaning? As I wrote furiously to capture the thoughts and feelings, the image of the Cheshire Cat came into my mind. The cat, with its symbolic smile of hidden knowledge, appears and disappears whilst 'hanging over' the proceedings, and is feminine by tradition, a representation of both transformation and compensation for patriarchal one-sidedness. I imagined my supervisor as coming into view as opposed to disappearing. This image and the words I had written fused together as a process of psychological resuscitation. What was also strikingly different about this supervision was that there was absolute unity in how members expressed the themes of this supervision through their thoughts. Unusual, as the process was often about expressing many different self states in expressing conflict arising from a client's story. This time, there was a general reaction of anger: a collective sigh that built up into a palpable growling roar.

Relational theoretical perspective

In the following discussion I integrate relational theories which seemed most relevant to me following on from this experience.

Holding vs containing

The differentiation is that *holding* provides the environment (Winnicot, 1965) and *containing* is the mother processing the affects of her infant (Bion, 1984), and that both processes overlap. Rather like mothers tolerating and surviving the infant's primitive attacks, by containing Marisa's attacks she needed to see me as an authentic external object, enabling the dual processes of maturation and development. The concept of holding shifts us from the concrete to the symbolic, enabling the therapist to take on the unbearable parts of their clients until such time as the client is ready for the return of the metabolised feelings. Failure to do so can result in the re-introjection of unmodified feelings to the client before they can take them in. Symington makes a useful distinction between *reacting* and *responding*, describing reacting as an inability 'to think one's own thoughts because of being forced into thinking someone else's thoughts'. In order to respond 'therapists must metabolise the affects of the patient sufficiently so that they can think their own thoughts and speak to the patient from a cognitive and affective centre within themselves rather than from a projected part of the patient' (1990, p. 74). He emphasises that we may have to react before we respond.

We are reminded by Gabbard and Wilkinson (1994) that, in receiving projective identification of the disavowed part of the client's self into the therapist, the essential part is the processing/containing element, and it is this which enables the therapist to re-introject in a reorganised way for the client. Davies and Frawley identify three explicit and implicit messages that the therapist communicates to the client: '(1) the clinician can bear the intensity and confusion of the patient's unsymbolised experiences; (2) unlike the original trauma, the patient is not alone now; (3) therapist and patient together can eventually symbolise the currently formless' (1994, p. 151). They also emphasise how important it is for the therapist not to abandon patients emotionally, thereby repeating the past in the present. Relating to the unsymbolised experiences, Gabbard and Wilkinson describe the capacity of the therapist to hold and contain, that 'the twin processes of holding and containment transform therapists in such a way that they can respond rather then react' (1994, p. 76).

Mentalisation

'Mentalising refers to making sense of each other and ourselves, implicitly and explicitly, in terms of subjective states and mental processes' (Allen and Fonagy, 2006, p. 185). This process is ongoing throughout our lives and 'enables us to learn and grow through relationships, including psychotherapy relationships' (ibid., p. 21). They encapsulate Bollas' insightful 'unthought known', which is the process of a client being unable to organise her early experiences into words – that she has, as of yet, been unable to think of them. 'In the absence of a containing mother, or where there is little ability to tolerate frustration … the outcome will be excessive projective identification [and] a deficit in the capacity for mentalising' (1987, p. 37). On thinking about Marisa's subjective states, her mother did not protect her from the abusive father and therefore her terror. Modells' writing on André Green's 'dead mother syndrome' relates the syndrome to 'the child's response to a traumatic disruption of maternal relatedness in … early childhood' (1999, p. 76). Given her story, Marisa's response told me much about her terror and how she could not make sense of our relationship. This encapsulates where we had become stuck in our rupture, our 'reciprocal lock'. What could unlock the grip we found ourselves in was me using the minds of the group: 'Awareness of others' mental states enables us to interact effectively, and explicit mentalisation … is essential for interpersonal problem solving' (Allen and Fonagy, 2006, p. 20). This means we can be receptive to the minds of others, open to their influence and able to take another's perspective. The supervision both facilitated my understanding of my part in this process and Marisa's potential new comprehension of herself. 'Just as a mother transforms the primitive anxieties of her baby through the process of her own reverie, therapists must metabolise the affects of the patient sufficiently so that they can think their own thoughts' (Gabbard and Wilkinson, 1994, p. 74).

Aspects of the third

What was named in the supervision group was the process of opening the space for the third, which in turn empowers us to simultaneously separate and connect. Benjamin's writings refer to the third as 'a quality or experience of intersubjective relatedness that has as its correlate a certain kind of mental space' (2004, p. 7).

The invaluable function of the third is that it enables us to move from the binary position (whether it be victim or guilty party, do-er or done to, sadist or masochist) and thus move from the complementarity position into a dialectic approach. Through the experience of an intersubjective mental space, we can take in the other's reality or point of view. What was needed was for both Marisa and I to survive the rupture, which in turn would open up a dialogue between us so we could begin to have a mutual meaning-making of what had happened: 'The experience of surviving breakdown … and subsequently of communicating dialogue – each person surviving for the other – is crucial to therapeutic action. From it emerges a more advanced form of thirdness, based on … the symbolic or interpersonal third' (Benjamin, 2004, p. 10).

She also reminds the clinician of the moral third, in which they are able to acknowledge their role in a rupture rather than thinking they are the one responsible for its repair. The supervision group had given me a different perspective, new ears and eyes on the rupture and reminded me that 'in relational thinking, an important sign of re-opening thirdness is being restored to the capacity to hear multiple voices' (Benjamin, 1990, p. 442). The clinician's acknowledgement and acceptance of their role demonstrates a 'sense of solidity that can tolerate scrutiny by the other, to transform the complementary see-saw of blame and invite the patient to … develop her own sense of agency and responsibility' (ibid., p. 450). We could move from the binary into what I saw as the four Rs: rupture, recognition, repair and restoration of the intersubjective space.

Gender, power and authority

It is important that Alice is a heroine, as she counteracts the infinite male child heroes in traditional Western literature, which have emphasised the masculine at the sacrifice of the feminine. I think it is significant that both the supervision group and the supervisor are all female, and that in Carroll's underworld, the most powerful characters are female, patriarchal values are upended and Alice learns to cultivate both 'male' and 'female' functions. She embodies the 'feminine' principle (Eros) with the 'masculine' principle (Logos) as expressed through her thinking function. Eating and drinking (as in the bottle that says 'Drink me' or the cake that says 'Eat me') in the book are also symbols of power. Alice is finally whole when she works out how much to eat.

Frawley-O'Dea and Sarnat's work on gender, power and authority refers to the role that gender plays within relationships and the polarisation of the nature of the sexes, that we can have fixed gender identity and that it is essential to attend to the theme of authority, as opposed to the 'restraining bonds of gender socialisation' (2001, p. 102). My supervisor had attuned to the fact that in feeling anxious about my client, I was avoiding my own self-assertion, thus doing myself and my client 'an equal disservice' (ibid., p. 101).

In connecting with 'authoritative narrative', Holloway and Wolleat (1994), as well as Slavin (1998), reiterate the intersubjective view that power belongs to the relationship (power *with* not power *over*) and is not the property of one individual or gender. Benjamin's feminist theories around the themes of domination reminded me that we can be binary in thinking about the roles of female/male, that we need to be assertive with each other as human beings and that we all express aggression – it is not under sole ownership of the male, and the female is not just a binary love/hate object. Benjamin's master-slave paradigm offered potential clues as to Marisa's way of relating to males and females, both intra-psychically and interpersonally: 'pattern[s] of domination ... set in motion by the denial of recognition to the original other ... The resulting structure of subject and object (gender polarity) thoroughly permeates our social relations, our ways of knowing' (1988, p. 220).

In examining the binary positions of sado-masochism, Benjamin's (1988) theories offer a way of understanding Marisa's apparent obedience to her supervisor. Benjamin departs both from a drive-orientated Freudian account of masochism as aggression turned inward and from feminist accounts of women as unwilling victims of male domination. She views sado-masochism through the lens of intersubjectivity, which considers the self-other dyad from two different perspectives simultaneously. Marisa was wrestling with the constant tension of needing the other for her own sense of self. Stark states that

> if the patient is ever to transform her sadism into a capacity to harness her aggressive energy in the interest of protecting herself from being violated, then the therapist must be comfortable with the idea that she herself ... might have the capacity to be relentless.
>
> (1999, p. 273)

The paradoxical dependence on others for our own sense of self was the core of the problem. If we destroy the other, there's no one left to recognise us, but there's no way of avoiding the danger that the other can destroy us. Benjamin refers to the balance within ourselves that is dependent on mutual recognition between ourselves and other, and says that there is real vulnerability when this element is missing in the process of differentiation. If the other cannot recognise us, our acts have no meaning, and conversely, as reflected in Marisa's story, if the other has so much power over us that we cannot change their attitude, we can only accede. There is no scope for self-agency, and so power can only be expressed in the dichotomy of obedience.

My response to the group process

Prior to supervision, it felt as if I had wordless thoughts. I thought of the parallel process in my supervisor sharing her mind in order to reclaim my own mind, proffering a bridge composed of words. Modelling through thinking and, more importantly, *being*, my supervisor had generated a psychotherapeutic torch to navigate my way in order to find Marisa. The losing/using myself in the group had bridged the potential chasm between us. In creating a different picture, I could now offer a different language to Marisa and be in a different psychic place in order to observeand offer her the essential reparative response: recognition.

Using a multiple set of functions, including reflecting on the client's internal object relations, self-analysis and verbal interpretations, the supervision offered me a transitional space of holding and containing in which to examine the subjectivities of my self and my client, I had moved from a mutual enactment into therapeutic reprieve. The connection with the minds in the supervision group facilitated the process of accommodation, co-creation and repair (Benjamin, 2004). Supervision had given me a 'corrective relational experience of bad-made-good' (Stark, 1999, p. 229). In thinking of relationship dynamics, Stark emphasises the transformational qualities in 'the curative power of the relationship itself … [which] involves authenticity, spontaneity, mutuality, reciprocity and collaboration' (ibid., p. 111). The holding supervisory environment modelled this, enabling me to contain what was being communicated to me via projective identification.

Further supervision reflections

Code signifier exercise

When I was writing this chapter, as I wrestled with how to capture the words, characters, images and metaphors within this story I felt like the White Rabbit, running around in search of something and someone. I explored in the group my counter-transferential writer's block through an exercise utilising a Lacanian approach of listening for signifying words, phrases and tones that are repeated and connected. Annie Rogers encapsulates this process beautifully in *The Unsayable* (2006), describing how she listens for the unspoken words by 'sieving' with a mental colander and catching key words and tones used in expressing those words which link to the client's unconscious processes.

Act One: I was asked to think of key words that summed up how I felt before the supervision, which were *madness* and *trickster*. I thought of Alice, the Mad Hatter and my self. I was then asked to think of a symbolic phrase, and came up with *two women in a tempest*. Shakespeare's *The Tempest* is about an island upon which the characters discover themselves, and this adventure had taken us into the Wonderland of the unconscious and the unknown. The many psychological miles Marisa and I travelled together had taken us directly to the eye of the storm.

Act Two: How did I see the supervision process? My two words to sum up the process: *power* and *feminine*. The key phrase that summed it up: *women round a cauldron*. The image of a Greek chorus came to mind, in the way that they would sum up themes in drama, and often expressed what could not be said by the actors to the audience, as well as their role of supplying characters with the insight they needed in order to avoid tragedy. Rather like the Furies, urging their heroine to safety, they represented the psychological antithesis to the Mad Hatter's tea party. There are many opposites in this story, from the black and white kittens to the Red Queen and White Queen, and just as Alice is the one who unites them, the supervision group had done this task.

Act Three: As I reflected on the process, how did I feel? There had been essential elements of opposites, magic, animals, power, transformation. The opposite aspects of Alice are represented in her personality (as illustrated by her talking with herself), and these need to be reunited. We see the splitting in Alice, when at one point she pretends to be two people, speaking in two different voices, yet making logical sense. This is crazy logic. In the nonsense underworld, all instructors (Humpty Dumpty, White Knight, Red and White Queens) offer guidance that is turned around and so, as in Hegelian terms, we learn from the positive element of determinate negation, they teach Alice by negative example. My two key words were: *relationship* and *relief*. The key sentence was: *Sitting on a lily pad*, a water version of the caterpillar on his toadstool. The caterpillar symbolises both death and rebirth; one of nature's most mysterious metamorphoses occurs when a caterpillar changes from a slow-moving creature to a colourfully winged, beautiful butterfly. I had exited Wonderland/supervision a changed person.

My task now was to begin a dialogue with Marisa: to move from binary complentarity into a dialectic position. Gabbard and Wilkinson emphasise the importance of 'verbal clarification of what is going on inside the patient and what is transpiring in the patient-therapist dyad' (1994, p. 78). We now had words.

'For there is nothing lost that may be found if sought'

'The idea, of course, is to be lost in the interest of being found at some later time' (Maroda, 2004, p. 56). I reflected that sometimes theory becomes poetic, as I found these words between my supervision and the next session with my client. Marisa arrived almost unable to speak, and certainly without her 'mind'. I began by asking her about her thoughts on what was happening; she replied she did not know. I asked her if she would like to know what was going on in my mind. She looked somewhat surprised and said 'yes'. I talked to her in a quiet and reflective way, beginning with the mentalisation process as discussed in the group. I spent some time telling her that I had been thinking about how far we had come together and how moved I was by that, and how I saw our work progressing: that we needed to have a forensic examination of what had happened both outside the room and within our therapeutic relationship in order to really understand the meaning of her story. At the end, I asked her what she thought of what I had shared with her. She looked at me for what seemed like an age and then began to cry. 'I didn't know how to separate it all... it feels so messy and I feel so angry and scared. I feel like I have just got my mind back for the first time in weeks. I just didn't know what was happening to me.'

I could feel that something alchemical had happened in the supervision process. By regaining a relational perspective (and dealing with my fearful fantasies) I had connected with what was curative for my client, which is described by Stark as 'the experience of finding and being found by, a therapist who is not afraid' (1999, p. 112). There was now the potential for Marisa and I to reconnect and to make meaning of what was happening between us, thus offering her the opportunity to have a new narrative. The recognition provided a movement from the victim/dominator role into 'a player mutually engaged with others, enjoying the meeting of minds' (de Young, p. 182).

I recalled Hargaden's 'When Parting is Not Such Sweet Sorrow' (2010), wherein she describes: 'I was like a blind woman who has suddenly regained her sight' – it really did feel like that for us both. In regaining my sight, I found both myself and Marisa.

This moment was truly a meeting of minds.

Conclusion

My experiences in supervision and writing this chapter have deepened my understanding of myself, my clinical work and the influence that the group and supervision holds in that process. The intersubjectivity of the group has encouraged me to use my own mind in conjunction with others to reflect upon my work. In trusting in my willingness to sit with what is unknowing and unspoken, rather than 'fix it' with actions or theories, my approach to my work has broadened.

The key themes of mutual recognition and self-agency within the intersubjectivity of the group emphasise the respect for self and the other. I see mutual recognition as a way of being more balanced within ourselves alongside a consideration of self with other and therefore a vital part of our professional and personal development.

I know that what emerges through the intersubjective and creative aspects of supervision can offer us transformational, and often magical, ways of connecting with our clients.

Chapter 7

Beyond thinking

Marion Umney

I have found writing this chapter challenging. Writing about something I have found difficult to describe in words has forced me to expand my thinking about communication and to accept that sometimes things are just not communicable in words. I have searched for ways to describe realms of intrapsychic and relational experience, the full flavour of which I found could only be approximated using the written or spoken word. It has seemed to me that there are several paradoxes in the work we do, including one concerning the nature of narrative. Psychotherapy is often referred to as 'talking therapy'. As a practitioner I know it is much more than that. It entails clients meeting themselves through their experiences, both past and present, and in a variety of realms: in affect, in body, in mind and in spirit. A significant part of my job is to help my clients make meaning of their past and their current experiences, and I generally would expect to do that through the symbolisation of words. Yet at times so much of that experience is unspeakable, either because it is too horrific or grotesque to be verbalised, or simply because it was experienced and introjected before we had words. It is either felt or dissociated but it has no verbal language and therefore can only be communicated through emotional or bodily reactions.

Over the years of my practice I have seen clients change and have recognised that their relationship with me has been instrumental in facilitating that change. I am aware that I have changed too. I learn from my clients and the impact they have had on me. Sometimes I have felt uncomfortable, not understanding what it was in me or the work that we did that enabled the client to change. At times I have also felt uncomfortable with the feelings clients provoke in me, and I have looked to find meaning in those feelings to ameliorate that discomfort. I have felt better if I could say 'It's OK. It's the client's material, it's not me,' or 'OK, I understand what it was that the client's material hooked in me. I can see my part and hers.' Whatever meaning I have made, my instinct has always been to search for understanding. I am aware this provides soothing and enables me to let go of or manage uncomfortable feelings. I recognise that, for me (and I suspect for others too), meaning-making is in the service of the client *and* myself. My feeling has always been that without words to make meaning of my experience, I would find the work impossible, and the toll that it would take would be too much.

The beauty and the difficulty of this process is that meaning-making, for me, has always occurred predominantly through language. The words may be concrete, reflecting theoretical analysis or descriptions, or they may be symbolic, using metaphors, stories or images. There are also non-verbal behaviours, reminiscent of proto-conversations, characterised by gestures, sighs, tears and body sensations. These aspects often reflect what is normally unconscious and the making of meaning is channelled through words which are coloured and given depth by affect, but are words just the same.

I am well educated and have a good command of language. I can find stories or metaphors to use with clients and supervisees with which they can identify and which they say represent what they are trying to convey. However, my experience with a client who struggled to articulate her story and with whom I had to rely heavily on body language and on my own intuition brought home to me just how much I relied on the spoken word. I knew I *could* engage with non-verbal material and had never had a problem doing so with the support of verbal confirmation; but in this case, the lack of a verbal narrative awoke in me an anxiety which created an impasse, the resolution of which required some close examination of my own defences. This is the story of my journey into that impasse through relational supervision in a group setting.

Narrative and meaning-making

Stephen Mitchell writes that 'we are our stories, our accounts of what happened to us', thus 'no stories, no self' (2002, p. 145), and cites research which indicates that narrative is the most fundamental way in which we make sense of our experience and so make sense of ourselves. He sees some kind of narrative process as primary in the development of an individual's sense of personal or cultural identity, and in the creation and construction of memories. Narrative has many constituent parts, but for adults these are generally clustered around thought and language which enable the construction of a story of the self, derived from what we know intrinsically about ourselves, what we are told, what we imply, assume and extrapolate. Personal narratives are necessarily co-created and change as we gather more information and experiences and as we test out our theories of ourselves. Narratives enable us to give structure to our experiences and to order and organise them in terms of their personal meaning (Emerson and Frosh, 2009). By applying narrative and giving language to our experiences we access different aspects of who we are and communicate them to others. In my psychotherapy work, my intention and expectation is that together my clients and I will be able to widen and deepen their knowledge and understanding of themselves. Their self-narratives will therefore develop and expand and the narrative will change as meaning and symbolisation happen in the therapy. The bad object (Klein, 1932), for example the poisonous mother, can be transformed and no longer have the same power over the client's internal world.

This change is achieved through my ability to pay attention to my client's narrative, to the verbalised story, the affect that is attached to the telling and my intuitive sense of the ulterior narrative, tested through careful questioning and my attention to my own bodily and emotional reactions. I particularly look for the potential influence of transference to inform me about my client and our relationship. I know that I will bring my own assumptions and interpretations, my frame of reference, to my speculations, and that as I learn more about the client those will change. I also know that I will become an aspect of her current self-narrative, as she will become an aspect of mine. We are both continuously changing and co-creating ourselves in relation to each other. All these things I have learned through my training, my professional development and my experience as a psychotherapist. Knowing is an abstraction with conscious and unconscious elements however, and through this process of relational supervision I have come to recognise that I have tended towards an attachment to the cognitive aspects of narrative, what Loewald (1977) would describe as the secondary process aspects of language. When there are no words and little in the way of behavioural cues, I am thrown back on intuition, what Loewald called primary process aspects (ibid.). My own lack of trust in those aspects and in my ability to find meaning and to communicate non-verbally has until now made it difficult for me to work as effectively as I might.

I can understand why. I come from a family where there was little space for anything beyond logic. My family origins were British working class and my parents had experienced hardship during the depression of the 1930s and the Second World War. The cultural wisdom, which they had imbibed and passed on, supported education as the way forward to a better life, with financial security as the goal. The ethic was work, and security was found in concrete, evidence-based thinking. Thinking was applauded; imagination and the esoteric were enjoyed but not valued, and intuition was mistrusted. My education was typical of the late 1950s and 1960s, and reinforced this pattern of relating to my mind, as teaching methods were rigid and science was valued above the arts and humanities.

Through my own therapy, one of the ways in which I have changed is learning to develop and trust my intuition, but it became evident that this was still insufficient when I was faced with a client who offered almost nothing in terms of a narrative, and I found myself deeply challenged.

The Inarticulate Speech of the Heart *(Van Morrison, 1983, cited in Hargaden and Sills, 2002)*

This title of Van Morrison's 1983 album was derived, according to Van Morrison himself, from a Shavian saying that refers to the idea of communicating with as little articulation as possible whilst at the same time being emotionally articulate. Hargaden and Sills (2002) have used this heading as the epigraph for their chapter on transference. They write that those familiar with Van Morrison's voice will understand that feeling of being moved without knowing why, and that 'Van Morrison transfers the inarticulate speech of his heart to us through his music' (p. 45). This spoke to me particularly strongly in the work I am about to describe.

Shortly after I joined the group I was asked to see a seventeen-year-old girl for psychotherapy. I will call her Lydia. The request came from Lydia's mother, but I was assured the appointment was being made at Lydia's request. Her mother told me nothing of Lydia's difficulties or her reason for seeking therapy, which was also my preference, as I wanted to form my own picture of my new client without any unnecessary influence from others. All I knew of her mother was that she herself was in psychotherapy with a colleague of mine, as that was the source of the referral.

Lydia arrived for our first appointment. She sat neatly on my sofa and was polite but appeared restrained and closed down. Her body language spoke of tight control. By contrast I noted her chipped nails, ragged cardigan sleeve and snagged tights, which suggested some chaos. She answered my questions with monosyllables or short sentences. She never failed to answer me, but she offered nothing. I learned little from her words and her non-verbal communication was also hard to read. She spoke slowly and carefully, in a voice that was quite high-pitched and verging on a drawl. She seemed younger than seventeen – more like fourteen or fifteen.

I was immediately disturbed by this young woman. I did not feel much warmth towards her, which is unusual for me. I felt confused and slightly irritated. The thought briefly crossed my mind that her presentation was all an affectation – the voice and the obsessive-compulsive behaviours she reported;

but underneath my irritation I felt something else which I could not get hold of. Was it fear? Was it rage? Was it desperation? It could have been any or all of those things, or none of them.

When she left I sensed she was as uncomfortable with the experience as I was. I wondered if she would come back, but she did. She continued to turn up for appointments, but no matter what I said, or how warmly I greeted her, her manner did not change. I began to dread the time of her appointment. I felt helpless. Whatever I tried, I could not get her to talk to me, and if I held the silence I sensed a rising discomfort between us. Very occasionally I would see a moment of vulnerability, but quick as a flash it was gone before I could establish any kind of connection with her. I felt as if the sessions were becoming a battleground between us: me trying to connect with her and her trying to stay away from me. It seemed this was a reflection of her internal battle, although I was unsure what this battle might be. I got the feeling that she wanted to connect with me; she wanted to be seen and heard, but could not allow that. Her stillness spoke of anxiety, vigilance, a need to control. She seemed frozen, and I was reminded of the story of Snegurochka, from Russian mythology, a magical child created by Father Frost who dies when her heart is warmed by the human emotion of love. Lydia's parents had divorced a few years earlier and, although the divorce appeared to be amicable and Lydia saw her father regularly, I wondered if she was afraid to feel love as that entailed loss, or maybe afraid to feel that other human emotion of anger.

These were just speculations however; underneath my thoughts I felt confused and helpless. I was faced with a client who offered almost nothing in terms of a verbal narrative, and I was experiencing surprise and disorientation. It was as if the ground had been taken from under my feet. What was I supposed to do with this? I had no starting point, no security, nothing concrete upon which to apply logic, or even informed speculation. My instinct told me to just sit with this, wait for something to emerge, but the absence of any dialogue between us felt uncomfortable for me, and I sensed it was uncomfortable for Lydia too. I had no idea what to say or how to be with her.

Lydia in the supervision group

The first time I took my work with Lydia to group supervision, I still saw myself as new in the group, and I was unsure of myself. This was a well-established group of highly qualified and experienced therapists, and I had not yet found my place. I felt completely lost with this client and a part of me was reluctant to share my helplessness with these people who, to me, seemed so self-assured and competent. What would they think? Would they come up with a clever solution? If they did I wondered if I would feel stupid for not being able to see that for myself, or if I would feel relieved that I now had a way forward.

In the early part of the session I noticed I was feeling irritated, along with another feeling which was difficult to describe. Immobilisation was the word which sprang to mind, and something a little more sinister – envy perhaps. A male member of the group, younger than me in years but very experienced and, to my eyes, self-assured, engaged for a considerable length of time with the supervisor. They were discussing an article and were clearly enjoying the discourse. One or two other people made contributions but the bulk of the discussion was between these two. I felt I had nothing of value to contribute. I felt isolated with my anxiety and feelings of inadequacy. It was only later that I registered I had projected my mother and my brother onto my supervisor and my colleague and had re-enacted the envy and iso-lation I had often felt as a child when observing their relationship. I also reflected that Lydia had a younger brother who had already been sent for therapy before she requested the same treatment. Was she conveying envy of her brother and a sense of isolation in her family through my transference in the group?

When it was my turn to bring my work with Lydia I chose not to use the Balint Chair option (a technique described in Chapter 1), but to ask for a group discussion. I had used the Balint technique before in exploring my work with another client, and although it had been extremely useful, I had not found it a comfortable experience. I was experiencing enough discomfort with this client; I did not want any more. In the Balint Chair I would be out-side of the conversation and powerless against the speculations of my peers. This time I was aware of a parallel with my client and registered the thought that perhaps she was afraid to be shamed if she exposed her thoughts and feelings to me. She too felt helpless and inadequate. Was I finding the client in myself?

The group were intrigued by my client. We talked a little about possible diagnoses and I was relieved that they were sympathetic to my dilemma. A variety of feelings were shared, practical suggestions were given and I felt reassured, calmed. I was interested that the man onto whom I had projected my envy was perhaps the most excited by and interested in my client. It was as if there was a liveliness (or aliveness) in him which was lacking in Lydia. I recognised that this was what I had noticed in his lively interaction with the supervisor. His attention and interest and that of my supervisor kindled a live-liness in me which I realised was missing in my interactions with Lydia. There was a flavour of play now as, in response to his energy, the group brought some laughter into the discussion, reflecting that teenagers often go through a toddler stage of stubbornness and intransigence, which could account for some of Lydia's behaviour with me.

Still with my thoughts on aspects of the client I might find in myself and noting my recognition of a lack of life in my relationship with Lydia, I reflected on André Green's concept of the dead mother complex (2001). In my own therapy I had identified a flavour of this in my history. My brother was born only a few months after my grandfather died and my grandmother came to live with us. I was just two years old. My mother had struggled to cope and needed to withdraw attention from me. In failing to find the mother I had lost I decathected (detached) from her and made her 'dead' to me. That rupture was repaired in time, but my unconscious identification with the dead mother, which is also part of the process of this complex, remained. I knew this in myself and understood my tendency to detach from people to avoid disappointment and the pain of loss. I wondered if Lydia had had a similar experience. Her mother was in therapy, although I did not know why, but I wondered if there was some trauma in the family which was at the root of Lydia's difficulties. She had experienced the loss of her parents' relationship through their divorce and admitted that she had been upset by that. She was now reaching a stage in her life when she would shortly leave home to go to university. Her inability to connect could be a reaction of deadness reflecting her fear of abandonment and the anticipated pain of loss, including the loss of me were she to attach.

What I took from the supervision was a sense of calm. I now had some speculative stories or narratives through which to start to understand something of Lydia's anxiety. The supervisor summed it up: 'She doesn't have a mind. She needs to use your mind in order to find her own. You have to tell her the story.' I would see if I could gain her trust through telling the stories I had mused on in this supervision, and so find the isolated, abandoned, fearful child in her. I decided I would do that through the use of play, as had been indicated by my colleagues and my supervisor in their interactions with me.

Looking back on that I am reminded of an article by Ray Little (2001) where, when considering how the therapist can reach the withdrawn Child ego state, he suggests that we remain curious and offer 'reverie' (Bion, 1962). This will open the door to our own understanding of what the client feels or wants and 'create a space in which they can experience love or hate' (Little, 2001, p. 39). However, in the same article Little reminds us that we must also be willing to sit quietly and not know what is happening. We need to walk the fine line between too much and too little.

The story continues

I continued to work with Lydia and invited her to use play materials with me. This was more comfortable for both of us. She needed to avoid my gaze, so I played alongside her. We used paints, sand trays and Play-Doh. She was a talented artist and was taking art at A-level, so she was comfortable with all these media. While our hands were occupied I would talk to her, creating narratives for her to digest or not. I sometimes asked her questions about herself and her life, or what she was creating. I got short answers, but at least I got something. I admitted my ignorance when she said she liked a particular music group or a book I knew nothing about, and hoped she might use her superior knowledge to start to talk. She did not. She just accepted my ignorance and remained silent. I gently speculated about pieces of her story which she *had* told me, using my counter-transference as a clue as to how she might feel about these events. For example, when I asked her to remind me how old she had been when her parents separated I noticed a feeling of sadness in me. Lydia answered in monosyllables as usual, but I used my feelings and said, 'It's really sad for kids when their parents split up.' This was directed at the room in general not at her. In this way I hoped she would hear that I understood she was sad, but would not feel intruded upon. I generally did not wait long for her to comment. I might just pause for a couple of seconds before moving on but I watched for any glimmer of a non-verbal response which might indicate I had stirred something in her. I could watch her out of the corner of my eye while we worked. She applied herself diligently to the task and rarely responded to my comments, either verbally or non-verbally. This included the thoughts I dangled in front of her about feelings of envy between siblings, or her sadness and anger about her parents' divorce and possible sense of isolation. All my efforts were apparently to no avail; she remained unmoved and unmovable.

When we finished whatever we were doing I made no attempt to find significance or meaning in what she had created. That would have felt clumsy and intrusive, and a lot of the time I did feel clumsy and intrusive with Lydia. I started to lose my confidence in the intuition I had gained through supervision. My anxiety about the lack of verbal communication in our interactions was returning so, in order to create some semblance of what felt to me like a relationship with her I might ask her, in mock grandiosity, 'So what do you think of this? What does it look like to you?' and show her my piece. As she speculated on what I had drawn or modelled I gained some understanding of how she saw me. She identified my depictions of emotions accurately; the crying child was sad, the fiery volcano was angry. I deduced that she was familiar with emotions – not as cold as I had sometimes imagined. I also sensed some sympathy from her at my clumsiness in drawing. I am no artist, and my figures were normally stick people. She was straightforward and factual in her responses, never suggesting any difficulty in identifying what I was attempting to depict as a result of my artistic incompetence, conveying respect for the process and my intentions. This helped me to see that the process *was* valued by her, and when I reflected on our progress, in spite of my bouts of anxiety, I realised I was becoming more comfortable with not knowing.

Using the Balint Chair

I eventually took my work with Lydia to the group again. By this time the supervisor had moved premises and the group membership had changed. Two groups had merged and I was the only member of my original group who was still there. In that sense I was a 'newcomer', but I had got to know the supervisor better and had experienced her respect for my work. I had allowed myself to take the risk of relationship with her. I also had friends in this group I had known in different forums and had already established relationships with, so I felt I had a place.

I decided to use the Balint Chair technique for this piece of supervision. The power of the Balint Chair for me is twofold: firstly the client case is normally presented without notes, which means that what is forefront in the relationship can generally be heard or felt through the order or the way in which the client is presented. Secondly, the therapist is 'outside' the supervision, looking in. She is discussed, along with the client as if she is not there, so she can focus on her own reactions without having to translate them into words in order to participate in the discussion.

My experience of this Balint Chair supervision was that the group did not seem to 'get her' as I had expected them to. Something in my presentation of her had highlighted a lack of understanding or of meeting. I felt she was evading them as I experienced her evading me. Then one member commented 'The stuck-ness is in Marion, not in Lydia.' I felt angry and frustrated. They were not getting me either. I could not say anything, as I was in the Balint Chair, so, like Lydia, I felt 'gagged'. I was gagged by the rules of the process. She was gagged psychologically by something; her trauma or her fear maybe. I was aware in a bodily sense, which is difficult to describe, that she did not speak because what was disturbing her was not something she could articulate. It was beyond verbal description. It was a feeling state for which she had no language. The best way I could describe it was a mixture of rageful impotence and fearful helplessness. I was not going to get the help I needed and I could not find a way to get through to these people who were supposed to help me. It was their fault ... no, it could not be their fault; it must be mine.

My supervisor's response to my colleague's comment was, 'Well, maybe, maybe not. Shall we see what she thinks?' and I felt relieved. I was not extricated from the group. It seemed there was a possibility I was going to be heard and understood. I found I could reflect on the remark and acknowledge that it had hit home, and I experienced extreme sadness. I agreed that I was probably evading Lydia, and I was also evading the fullness of what relational supervision could give me were I to allow myself to engage fully with the process. This was heard by the group and particularly by my supervisor, who reflected her experience of me in this group in contrast to the previous group – how much more at ease I seemed, and how much she was enjoying me. She suggested perhaps I role play the client and ask the group to role play me, and I laughingly agreed, enjoying her invitation to play with her and my colleagues. Lydia and I were now well and truly in the room, and I noticed the effort made by the group to understand her and to help. At the end of the supervision my supervisor invited me to comment on how that had been. After a moment's reflection I risked telling the group how touched I felt that they were really putting themselves out for me. They might not be able to give me the answers I wanted, but they cared and were offering me support and recognition – the warmth of an intimate relationship. My supervisor just said with a smile, 'Good. OK to move on now?' and we did.

Through this experience I had managed to move beyond thinking and had made meaning. I had got in touch with primitive feelings. I had felt I was not being seen or heard and I had experienced that feeling change through a tacit working through of my own transference onto my supervisor and the group. They had responded to my projected fear of abandonment by offering a relationship where they were willing to endure my frustration and stay in contact with me. In her closing interaction with me I realised that my supervisor had recognised the transference and was willing to work with it. It was a moment of intimacy between us.

I re-read Green's work on the dead mother (2001) and was struck by his reflections on the infant's dependency on the variations of the mother's moods. When the infant comes into contact with the deadness and inconsistency in the mother, Green describes the experience as being cruelly painful (p. 181), leaving the infant adrift, uncertain and dependent on guesswork and anticipation. He suggests that the unity of the ego is compromised by the inconstancy of mother. There is now a hole in it and the developing infant compensates for the damage either on the level of fantasy or on the level of knowledge. If he chooses fantasy he opens the door to artistic creation; if he chooses know-ledge, he opens the door to highly productive intellectualism.

I realised that my response to my own early experience of abandonment had been to rely on thinking and intellectualisation, hence my anxiety when I had little to support my guessing and anticipating. I am a transactional analyst, and a basic concept in classical TA is that of drivers (Kahler, 1975) – the Child ego state's answer to surviving in a family: 'If I am strong, if I am perfect, if I please others, if I try hard or if I hurry up they will love me.' The 'try hard' driver is prominent in my script (Berne, 1961), and I had often been told the challenge for this kind of presentation is to 'give up the struggle'. A trainer had reinterpreted this for me as 'Don't do … just be'. I realised I needed to 'trust the process', a phrase I had never really understood until that moment. Lydia would do what she needed to do with me in spite of my attempts to find out her story, not because of them.

After supervision

I did not radically change the way I was working with Lydia. We continued to use play materials as before, but I relaxed and started to enjoy our encounters. I stopped expecting anything from her and I stopped trying to persuade her to talk. I accepted that I was providing a good enough relationship, which might, in time, be the reparative relationship she needed. This therapeutic work would happen through an unconscious process between us that would be impossible to explain fully. I could model the containment I experienced in the group to maintain a safe, boundaried and respectful space for the work and allow Lydia to do what she needed to do with me in her own time and her own way. I could also allow myself to want an intimate relationship with her, rather than to fear it. I knew that if it did not happen I could bear the disappointment.

Lydia stayed for another three months then announced she was going to stop coming. I *was* disappointed. I had just started to enjoy her and to allow myself to care and now she was leaving. However something had shifted in me, and I knew I would survive this separation without needing to detach from what I felt for her.

I did not try to keep Lydia with me. This was *her* therapy and her choice. I did offer a last session for us to review our work together, to which she agreed. In that session I told her I was sad she was leaving and I would miss her. I think she heard my sadness, but did not offer any comment except a polite 'Thank you' and a shy smile.

A week or so later I received a letter from Lydia's mother and through this learned just a little. Her mother said Lydia was engaging with her more and that she (the mother), through her own therapy, was learning to stay connected to her daughter no matter what was being stirred in her. Her letter implied conflict and I was glad that Lydia had come to life in her relationship with her mother.

Reflections on relational supervision

My understanding of relational supervision is that it is an approach that follows the two-person (Stark, 1999) relational or intersubjective perspective in contemporary psychotherapy. Relational psychotherapists argue that behaviour is determined in an intersubjective field, also referred to as the psychological space or the analytical third, and that clinical treatment is co-created between the client and the clinician (Aron, 1996; Aron and Harris, 2005; DeYoung, 2003; Hadley, 2008, cited in Miehls, 2010). By the same token, relational supervision uses the intersubjective field between the supervisor and supervisee. In the case of a group the field is extended to include relationships between supervisees and between each supervisee and the supervisor. The supervisees' clients also come into the field as they are presented for supervision and, as Frawley-O'Dea (1998) notes, the supervisees' therapists may also be there in terms of transferential dynamics to the supervisor. The supervision is a co-created venture whereby each individual in the group is willing to engage in that intersubjective field and bring her own self – her perspective, her thinking and her honest responses – to what is happening in the supervision process. This requires a high degree of trust within the group and sensitive facilitation by the supervisor.

My understanding of a relational paradigm of supervision is that, like the contemporary model of relational psychotherapy, it is based on a higher degree of mutuality between supervisor and supervisee than traditional supervision. This needs to be co-constructed and may take time to evolve. Although this is a supervision group as opposed to a therapy group, it is accepted and agreed as part of the process that the group is a safe space within which we can touch on earlier forms of experience. This occurs through memories which are invoked, through connection with and release of emotion and, most importantly, through the differing transference relationships that emerge with other members of the group, the supervisor and the group as a whole (Pines, 1994).

Pines is referring to a therapeutic relationship; a supervision group is by necessity different, as the focus is different. Frawley-O'Dea, however, makes a case for some element of therapy or analysis being necessarily accepted in the supervision relationship, but with the focus on the professional development of the supervisee as opposed to their personal development. She suggests that supervision is enhanced and enriched when supervisor and supervisee are willing to collaborate and freely share 'the intricacies and vicissitudes of their own relationship as it takes shape' (1998, pp. 516–17). This paradigm then allows for mutually constructed parameters for their relationship and their work, which will include the supervisee's psychic processes.

Frawley-O'Dea is writing about the dyadic relationship of individual supervision, but the same applies to a group except that the mutual construction of parameters of relationship includes all group members and the supervisor. In my experience this adds further depth and richness to the transformational space created through the intersubjective field.

Group supervision of this nature supports increased scope for creativity and risk-taking, however the containment of that space is crucial if it is going to facilitate risk-taking within the group and allow for creativity. Sharing my responses to the Balint Chair supervision with the group was a risk I would not have taken had I not experienced the group as a contained space. My earlier experience of supervision on this client, while facilitating insight into my own and my client's process, was less transformational, as I was not experiencing the safety of containment in the group to the same extent. From this it is clear to me that the necessary containment evolves through increasing trust in all the relationships within the group. The supervisor has a crucial role here in maintaining a balance between control and fluidity. Control comes from the stated and unstated norms and boundaries within the group: confidentiality, mutual respect and the maintenance, as far as possible, of an environment where experiences of shame can be articulated and explored alongside acknowledgment of the real power and experience difference between the supervisor and the supervisees, which 'within the asymmetry of each relationship … is authorised rather than assumed' (Frawley-O'Dea, 1998, p. 516).

What I find invaluable in relational group supervision is the focus on relationships, including my relationship with myself, and the ways in which unconscious processes may be experienced through transference and multi-level parallel processing. All these provide opportunities for multiple, lateral meaning-making. There is permission, within the relational framework of the group, to have no answer – to have a feeling, physical or emotional, and to have no explanation as to what this might mean. There is also the opportunity and support to explore multiple meanings. Group process as opposed to the individual supervision dyad opens up the transformational space. Even when, as occasionally happens, the group does get into dyads, I have experienced the supervisor's insistence upon reflective processes and the incorporation of different self-states, as facilitating a move to a different place of meaning or multiple meanings. My increasing understanding of my work with Lydia and its significance would not have developed without the different insights of the group members or the multiple transferences I experienced with them.

Unformulated experience and language

Since my work with Lydia I have become more interested in the role of language in our sense of identity and in how we work with clients and ourselves to explore the unconscious. Winnicott (1975/1945) proposed that, at our core, we remain unknown even to ourselves, and we know that much of what transpires in psychological space, or the intersubjective field, is unconscious. Much later, Donnel Stern (2003), who first used the phrase 'unformulated experience', suggested that thought originates, often unexpectedly, from somewhere behind consciousness – beyond thinking. Winnicott (1975/1945) also proposed that there are elements that exist in the unconscious which have never been organised and others which have been organised but have now become disorganised, possibly through trauma. The elements that are unorganised and exist as what we now term as unformulated experiences are normally understood to be preverbal, and therefore inaccessible to language and to cognitive thinking processes. Rather, they are experienced as amorphous affects, which may take the form of feelings, urges, impulses, anxieties or images. Heller (2010) notes that artists are very good at using unformulated experience, and often lose interest in their project when it is complete; it is the process which is important.

Daniel Stern was also fascinated by the richness of early experience. For him the advent of language was a mixed blessing. As a mode of communication it made possible what Stern referred to as the generation of 'the sense of a verbal sense' and the opening up of 'a new domain of relatedness' (1985, p. 162). He regards language as a double-edged sword. On the one hand it creates a divide between forms of interpersonal experience: the experience as we live it and the experience as we represent it through language. So for Stern language is the cause of 'a split in the experience of the self' (ibid.). On the other hand, Stern also recognises the value of language in its ability to move relatedness away from the personal, immediate level and into the realm of the impersonal and abstract, thus allowing for an entirely new level of thinking and understanding.

Stephen Mitchell (2002) has written an interesting review of the work of Loewald (1977). He writes that Loewald suggests that this distinction is misleading, and that language is present from birth. The child is surrounded by language, but initially words are experienced as sounds embedded in dense, undifferentiated experience. Later, these same sounds, words, become infused with semantics and this function takes precedence over their sensual, affective features. Loewald refers to this as language in primary process and language in secondary process. The question is what happens to the primary process experience of language when its use is superseded by the secondary process of meaning-making. According to Mitchell, Loewald seems to suggest that, as language develops, a deep link between the child's sensory affective experience of language and its adaptive everyday form remains. To my way of thinking this might explain the idea of the 'Freudian slip', where unconscious ideas enter discourse through slips in the use of language. It may also go some way to account for the Lacanian idea of 'signifiers' as offering a signal to what is waiting to be discovered in the unconscious, illustrated so delightfully by Annie Rogers in *The Unsayable* (2008).

Mitchell also writes about what Loewald suggests happens when that linkage is inadequately balanced. According to Mitchell, Loewald's view is that if the abstraction is insufficient the child may remain entangled in something of an autistic state, unable to link language and affect, but if language is drawn too much into secondary process and the link is not maintained, the result can be functional competence at the cost of an affectively dead and empty existence. Loewald says nothing about what might predispose one to these maladaptive transitions, but for me this resonates with the dead mother complex: a child's attempt to separate from feeling by replacing affect with thinking and intellectualisation.

Conclusion

For those of us working within the relational paradigm and even for those who are not explicitly doing so, a deepening of our capacity to sit comfortably with not knowing seems to be essential to professional development. In their reflections on relational supervision Boyd and Shadbolt (2011) suggest that self-reflection in supervision is the route to deepening our notion of parallel process. My understanding of the way in which they use this term is that it is not the sometimes clichéd way it is often used. What they describe are the transferential dynamics between client and therapist often repeated between therapist and supervisor, which lead to the possibility of a reparative relationship for the client. In relational supervision they see such self-reflection as inclusive of a range of thoughts, both the supervisor's and the supervisee's, and a range of experiences and disturbances. They regard all of these as 'vital to the transformational potential of relational … supervision' (p. 283).

There is plenty of space here for recognising that in the intersubjective field co-created in relational supervision there is recognition and respect for intuition and for not knowing. In this process, and particularly where the richness of the group is added, I have found a greater transformational potential than in traditional supervision. My experience has confirmed that, as Benjamin (2002a) suggests, it is the therapist who has to change in order to create the space which allows for the emergence of what has been hitherto unknown.

When I reflect on myself and my practice prior to participating in this group I see a competent-enough, solid practitioner. When I reflect on myself now, I see a practitioner who is willing to risk not knowing, to risk discomfort, to reflect on my own part in whatever is happening between myself and my client and to explore creative ways of being with that client. I believe I am more effective and more alive in the work. I love the intellectual side of myself. I like my ability to think, to rationalise and to analyse, but I am also reconnecting with my intuitive side, which in Jungian terms would be described as a part of my shadow – elements of my psyche which I have sublimated or disavowed. This means really allowing myself to feel the impact of others, without avoiding the potential pain of intimacy, within the group, in my work with clients and in my personal relationships. I have come to believe the work I was doing previously was not fully relational, even though I was using my counter-transference and allowing myself to be affected by that. How could it be if I was unable to tolerate the risks in relationship?

This learning and process of change is not always comfortable, as demonstrated by the experience I have described in this chapter, but it has been worth the discomfort.

Chapter 8

Shame

Helena Hargaden

In this chapter I discuss the nature of shame, giving several examples of how it operates in ourselves and within systems. From these experiences and observations I consider the reasons why it is important for us as therapists and supervisors to be conscious of our own potential to connect to shameful self states. I describe the destructive effects of disavowal of these feelings, such as victim rage, defensiveness and projection. However, when such feelings are acknowledged, when there is a focus on building resilience in ourselves and others, I show how it becomes easier to create the space where healing and transformation is possible.

What is shame?

Shame is often described as pathological. Gabbard (1992) describes it as linked to either over-sensitive narcissistic types or grandiose hyperbolic types. The danger of this categorisation is that it may lead us to think that as psychotherapists we are somehow immune to it. Within relational work however, with an understanding of the bi-directionality of unconscious relatedness, we cannot avoid the experience.

Shame is thought to be linked to narcissism (Jacoby, 1994) and the feelings of low self-esteem which lurk beneath the surface of self-aggrandisement. Shame can attach itself to most things, and is often used to control others. An obvious and immediately recognisable area in which this control operates is in the massive cultural forces aimed at dominating womens' behaviour by attempting to shame them, in every realm of their existence – for not being good enough mothers, wives, daughters, carers or lovers (de Beauvoir, 1949/2014). Some may think it has even worsened in a post-feminist age where women have dared to go beyond these roles and are now criticised for not having children, being too sexual, not sexual enough, eating too much, not eating enough, etc. A woman inclined to own her authority is referred to as 'bossy'. Aging has almost become a criminal offense, the punishment for which is invisibility (women disappear from film, TV and public life after a certain age). Recently a politician complained that some women didn't clean behind their fridges! Although the comment was viewed as laughable, it was symbolic of an underlying misogynistic attitude inherent in the culture about who and what a woman should be and how shamed she will be if she fails to live up to these implicit and invariably contradictory standards. These ideas are unconsciously internalised, and are frequently used by women to punish themselves when they fail (as inevitably they must) to live up to these ideals of themselves, as described in the following example.

A female colleague described her sense of shame when she bumped into her client at an airport. My colleague's husband was struggling to get through security, having mislaid his boarding pass, when her client appeared out of nowhere, greeting her warmly. My colleague was disconcerted, as she was trying to help her husband whilst also being aware of professional boundaries, so replied with a smile, but immediately turned away to deal with the boarding-pass issue. Later she described feeling some shame that she had been too brusque with her client. In our conversation it became clear that the feeling came from having set a boundary that made her feel uncomfortable because she felt it would be perceived as uncaring. Although cognitively she understood all the reasons and arguments for boundaries, and could probably have written a thesis on it, this did not prevent her from feeling shame, which we thought was linked to her idealisation of herself as a carer and a giver, a compassionate and warm woman. By setting the boundary (so brusquely in her terms) she became ashamed of her so-called 'masculine' qualities, characteristics which she had had to subjugate as a child in order to ensure that her relational needs were met. Through discussion it emerged that her experience mirrored a fundamental process in her client, with whom she had only had two sessions. The client had unreasonably been accused of not being good enough, caring enough, warm enough by a dissatisfied patient in her place of work. This had put the client into a state of anxiety and self-doubt, the roots of which were found to be in a narcissistic and punitive father who humiliated his daughter mercilessly.

Shame has a destabilising effect on a situation; it feels so shocking to our cognitive understanding that our minds temporarily freeze. This is especially so since it is so difficult to understand when there is often no rational reason for it, just a sense that one has gone against standards previously internalised and long since forgotten, or memories which seem quite banal when we recall them yet once were riven with shameful feelings. For example, I remember feeling shamed by my parents that I had acquired an English accent and lost my 'lovely' Irish accent. I recall my anger at the absurdity of their complaint, and defiance, with which many an immigrant's offspring will readily identify. I felt an unaccountable feeling of shame which was undoubtedly linked to their need for me to be 'perfect' for them, and their shame when I was not. They were impervious to my need to belong, leaving me with not only shame but its close companion, isolation.

Why shame?

Shame is the poor relation of affective process. Who wants it? No one probably, and yet we all need it. Mencius (a Chinese philosopher) says that

> Men cannot live without shame
> A sense of shame is the beginning of integrity …
> (quoted in Zhou, 2007)

Mencius is right, for shame has a natural place in our psyche, acting as a 'prohibitive, inhibitory, and reactive counterforce to the pleasure principle' (Schore, 1994, p. 200). To this extent shame is a developmental and necessary process which regulates our behaviour, making it possible for us to co-exist in the world. More corrosively shame has the power to create 'walls of secrecy' (O'Loughlin, 2009, p. 54), behind which people suffer in isolation. Jacoby (1994) refers to the archetype of shame, meaning that a pattern of feeling exists in the collective unconscious, ready to be evoked at any point in the environment.

Wounds of shame

Michael Eigen sees shame as attached to pain: 'We think pain is only private and [we] withdraw [from it]. So much childhood pain goes unanswered or misunderstood. People are afraid of each other's pain and their own, helpless, not knowing how to respond to the pain of life' (Eigen, 2006b, p. 29). We can understand this description of pain as trauma, which is described in Chambers as 'an emotional wound or shock' (p. 1660). Jung described trauma as the avoidance of legitimate suffering. Thus the trauma is hidden in self-states and cannot be consciously known; it is an experience from which the person dissociates. Many clients or patients, alongside psychotherapists and counsellors, have either experienced trauma or have inherited unconscious trauma from their parents (Hargaden, 2013b; Jacobs-Wallfisch, 2013). As Eigen suggests, trauma is impregnated with shameful feelings, and the disavowed shame is often passed on through projective identifications (Shaw, 2014). Since non-verbalised experience can only emerge through the co-created unconscious relational dynamics between therapist and client, it follows that ruptures and enactments are an inevitable part of the therapeutic and supervisory process, making it impossible to avoid these feelings.

Not everyone reading this will have been wounded so consciously 'by the shrapnel of shame' as those who have been exposed to cultural hatred (Corbett, 1996, p. 458; Shadbolt, 2009). Self-hatred induced by societal attacks causes massive amounts of psychological pain: 'such experiences have a corrosive effect on the psyches of individuals and communities' (O'Loughlin, 2009, p. 135). Most commonly shame is hidden in the unconscious, a response to cumulative emotional trauma in childhood. When children are raised by neglectful, depressed or narcissistic parents, who fail to mirror the subjectivity of their child, self-agency and selfhood are severely compromised. This leads to feelings of shame at any sense of having needs and being seen as a vulnerable dependent person (Shaw, 2014). In Chapter 5, Gina Sweeting uses the metaphor of Narcissus and Echo to demonstrate the damaging effects on our work in supervision and therapy when we have a compromised and shame-based sense of our subjective self.

Most importantly though, would any of us be in this profession without our own painful legacy of shame? Many of us were attracted to this work because we wanted to understand more about how we had been hurt. Perhaps it is our willingness to know ourselves in the most shamed parts of experience that enables us to offer true compassion to our clients. It has often been observed that the very nature of therapy, supervision and training is rife with opportunities for shaming, because it is an inevitable part of relatedness, which is why we mostly try to avoid it. How easy then for our disavowed shame to be projected onto clients and patients, supervisees and students.

Shame as a contagious and controlling process – 'the hot potato!'

In the following episode I describe how shame, when it emerges in someone, can be passed around like a hot potato (English, 1969), projected outwards, defended against, until it finds somewhere to land.

I became more conscious of my vulnerability to catching the 'hot potato' of shame when, many years ago, I was an examiner on a mock exam board for a candidate preparing for her teaching and supervising transactional analysis examination. The candidate was a qualified and experienced psychotherapist, and because of this I anticipated that she would be resilient and able to engage with quite challenging ideas, since this was the purpose of the exam: to demonstrate a robust and sophisticated level of understanding at a theoretical and practical level. With this in mind I asked her how she thought about, and engaged with, cultural differences. In those days it was still quite a novelty to think about the relevance for example of race, class, sexuality and gender in the therapeutic sphere. It was as if the psyche was in a special compartment all of its own, sealed off from other influences in what O'Loughlin describes as 'unexamined representations of otherness' (2009, p. 118). The candidate was taken aback by my line of questioning. When she became quite defensive as I attempted to talk her through it, acknowledging that this might be new territory for her, I began to feel uncomfortable, at which point I now can see that we were both feeling controlled by the emergence of shame between us. The exam situation is a natural context for such feelings to emerge, because the candidate is under scrutiny.

Shame easily segues into anger and even rage as a way of deflecting the acute sense of powerlessness at its heart. The candidate's way of dealing with her feelings was later to complain to her supervisors (who held quite powerful positions in the teaching institute to which I belonged) that I had deliberately sought to shame her. As can happen in institutions, I was informed on the grapevine about what I had 'done'. It even seemed to me that culture was in itself a shameful subject, not to be discussed. When examining my vulnerability to pick up such projections of others' disavowed shame, I began to explore my Irish Catholic background, in my Jungian analysis. As my narrative unfolded of catastrophic ancestral experiences and the extent of the transgenerational trauma I carried, shame seeped through every conversation. Shame is hidden in silence. In Ireland there is still resistance to talking about the famines, when Ireland lost approximately twenty-five per cent of its population (O'Loughlin, 2009). When referring to the Holocaust Benjamin describes the overwhelming trauma to a people who have experienced a 'psychic insult', and the shameful affects associated with the experience of such violent and evil hatred; this captures the Irish experience exactly, an understanding of which helped me reflect on why I had unconsciously carried such a burden of shame.

The sense of powerlessness in any shamed person is experienced as threatening (Gerson, 2009). Not only had the candidate felt powerless, but the supervisors, as representatives of the institution, also felt implicated, threatened by what may be perceived as their ignorance and inadequacy. How to reinstate power both in the candidate, and the institution? Pass it on. I had become a scapegoat for disavowed feelings of shame which was interlinked with the subject that I had unwittingly raised, that of cultural identity. I was vulnerable to taking this position because of the transgenerational trauma hidden in my family background. Shame had originally been constellated not only in the student, but also in the system of the organisation, which had fallen into the shadow of its imperfection – a shadow that had its roots in the organisation's shameful cultural heritage that had never been fully acknowledged. In this way the disavowed shame of both student and system were projected onto me. Shame is linked to vulnerability, weakness and inferiority and, most inhumanly of all, causes a severe sense of isolation. No wonder we want to disavow it.

Ruptures in supervision – leaving space for the light to get in

We are concerned here with the effect of these dynamics in supervision. As already noted, our involvement in this profession is rooted in our own injuries, so we are likely to have dissociated aspects of self, no matter how much therapy we do. Rather similar to Jung's idea, referred to above, is Donnel Stern's observation that dissociation is not about an experience from which we cut ourselves off, or repressed because it was too painful, but an affective experience which was too difficult ever to allow into our consciousness in the first place (Stern, 2004.). It follows then that ruptures and enactments are the vehicle by which such dissociated experience come into consciousness. Indeed it is our clients who will show us more about ourselves than anyone else. They will unwittingly take us to the places we do not know about, and do not want to know. Thus, supervision given by therapists involves us all in a sensitive area of enquiry into not only the heart of the client, but the darkness at the heart of the therapist and the supervisor.

The supervision sessions described in this book have often been highly charged and intense. Some members could not deal with this situation unless they returned into therapy. See Brian Fenton's powerful description in Chapter 2, describing, as did others, how he did not feel safe enough, yet when he went into a deeper analysis of his internal world he developed resilience. Through the personal accounts in this book it has become clear that an essential part of the journey is to allow for this affective experience and to understand it as the route through to aliveness – to avoid it is to stay in the deadness.

Learning how not to be a good therapist

Part of the teaching in a relational supervison group is learning how the 'good enough' therapist has to learn to let go of perfection, to allow for mistakes, to make way for the unconscious. For some this means not feeling good enough. Nevertheless the learning involves finding out that the value of enactment in the therapeutic process (see vignette in Chapter 1), is that it can create the space for healing. It is through this process that unformulated experience can emerge into the relationship, be metabolised and become a part of consciousness. The main point about an enactment is that we do not know we are in it. Once we become aware of it we are likely to feel many difficult feelings, such as rage, envy, frustration, anger, guilt and shame. Stern suggests that such experiences are reminders of the mystery of living, that we are only human and that we cannot avoid such dynamics by an act of will (2004). Teaching and learning in this way about the links between shame, trauma, enactment and ruptures strengthened the minds of each person in the supervision group and created a strong container for group processes.

Creating the conditions to feel and think about shame

The supervision group not only provides the potential for the therapist to discover that she has been in an enactment but the group itself has the potential to be involved in an enactment. One of the benefits of group supervision is that when one member feels vulnerable and overexposed, we all share in that feeling in some way, thus creating a 'mutual third'. By working through it collectively the part of each person which is dissociated, shame-based or defensive is affected in the process. In this way it becomes more possible to share the most negative and difficult feelings because of the implicit understanding, based on previous experience in the group, that there will be no ritual humiliation, or superior 'knowledge' brought to the situation, but more a co-created, compassionate and reflective understanding based on an attempt to get to 'the bottom of things', whilst accepting that we may not. See Heather Fowlie's graceful narrative reflecting this process in Chapter 3.

Within such a human context, the potential for ethical practice is increased as the therapist is less likely to unconsciously project her own unmetabolised contents onto the patient or client. The value resides in observing and experiencing other therapists and colleagues willing to be open and non-defended. In such an environment we do not rely on the embalming effects of masterful theories or confine the client to a pathological description such as stating that 'Well, she is borderline/narcissistic/schizoid/hysterical'. These descriptions of course can be useful, but only when we acknowledge how that part of the client/patient is sequestered in parts of our self. And, as always, when we find this within ourselves, we find it within each other. Sharing, witnessing this in each other, provides an atmosphere of mutuality, reciprocity and aliveness.

Vitality is the enemy of shame. It breaks through the deadening experience and opens up the possibility for hope, that what once was ugly and contempt-ible can be transformed into something beautiful, and in the case of the person who feels the shame, into someone who is lovable.

Throughout this book the underlying theme of this relational approach is that unless the therapist is able to be vulnerable, able to be changed, open to surprise, fundamentally nothing will change. One of the paradoxical aspects of our work is that the more senior and experienced we are, the more removed we can become from our vulnerable selves. How tempting it can be, and easy it is, to hide behind our theories and expertise. Perhaps continuing profes-sional development is as much about finding the space to remind ourselves of this vulnerability as it is about learning new ways to think, which of course is also valuable.

Chapter 9

Analysis of my experience in starting and developing relational supervision groups

Helena Hargaden

In Chapter 1 I outlined my relational approach to supervision. In the ensuing chapters former and current members of groups have written reflective accounts of their experience, describing how they have developed as therapists, situating their own unique perspectives on relational work within the context of supervision. In this chapter I describe my experience of the process of setting up and running relational supervision groups. Although I refer to 'the group', I am including several groups with which I have worked in this way.

Difficult times

The spirit of adventure that launched us on our initial relational supervision journey soon ran into rocky waters. Some members of the group reported feeling overwhelmed by the uncensored intensity of responses to their presentation of clinical material. Recognising that the process was too shame-inducing and bewildering to be clinically useful, I suggested we alter the structure (as set out in the five phases of the supervision approach described in Chapter 1) to enable the presenting therapist to preserve a sense of her own authority and agency. Instead of sitting in the group, the therapist would now sit outside, as an observer, and make her own notes about our process.

Whilst this boundary created a more secure situation there was a related issue that could not be resolved by structural change. Still some people continued to find the method of free associative feelings and thoughts too threatening of their reality, in a way which could not be contained. This had the effect of closing down the group process as, understandably, there was a reluctance to offend anyone or put themselves into the firing line by saying the 'wrong' thing. The group's natural default position was to revert to the safer and more traditional and detached methods of group supervision with which they were familiar.

I realised that at this stage of the group's development my role was to model the relational process I wanted to instigate. I could not expect the group to reveal their vulnerability whilst I sat, like a Buddha, detached and idealised as the 'perfect' observing ego. This involved me in the delicate business of immersing myself in the 'here and now' intersubjective process whilst retaining my ability to observe and reflect on what was happening. It felt rather precarious, as I had to (temporarily) forgo the traditional care-taking role of the 'good' supervisor and instead voice feelings and thoughts that ran counter to the implicit expectations upon us as supervisors that we be more detached in our understanding. I realised that I could only teach the group that it was possible to be vulnerable in this way, without losing my professional sense of self, if I was willing to become an involved participant. When I openly expressed feelings and thoughts that emerged directly in response to the presentation, without being mindful of how those expressions might sound or be received, others followed. We began to observe how direct expressions of affect opened up the emotional valves which led us directly into darker disturbances – not as a cognitive understanding, but as a breathing feeling reality in the room. There was a shared sense that the emotional disturbance in the room belonged to us and not only to the client. This process is captured by a participant in relational group supervision who wrote an account of her experience for a booklet on relational supervision which can be found on the IARTA website, as follows:

> I find that the most surprising feelings can emerge as if from nowhere if I stay with my own process. Strong feelings of fury, boredom, irritation, sadness, inappropriate amusement and disgust have not been unusual, all of which provide useful clues to the emergent unconscious process.
>
> (Lee, 2008, p. 23)

By letting go of the urge to 'make sense' of everything, and in making space for the dialectical interplay of conflicting realities, we learned two valuable lessons. One was the potential to find the rich meanings inherent in paradox The other was that the intersubjective experience, to which we all belonged and which we co-created, changed our experience. This is described as follows:

> Its seems that when it comes to expressing feelings anything is allowed. Sometimes there is a united feeling of 'eureka' within the group when

a client seems to be understood more clearly. However, often the group is divided by its contradictory feelings. The interesting thing is that the group feels like an entity at times, with a will of its own. There is a sense that the unconscious process is taking over. We are all 'learning to develop a type of stereophonic listening to the conscious and the unconscious, to the cognitive and the affective' (Cornell and Hargaden, 2005, p. 243). This is important when we are working relationally because as Novellino and Moiso (1990, p. 191) say 'intuitive understanding of the patient and of his or her unconscious is brought about through the unconscious of the therapist, who can understand another person's unconscious to the same degree that his or her own unconscious mind is able to accept his or her own unconscious reactions.

(Lee, 2008, p. 24)

In writing this, Lee captures the interplay between opposing forces, the interaction between experience and theory as it happens, and shows how she develops her clinical sensibility by paying attention to her own experience and making theoretical links.

Analysis of the difficult times

There was however continued resistance to this methodology. Some voiced concern that they did not feel safe; there were so many 'inappropriate' feelings being expressed that they felt protective of their client, that there was 'no need' for such negativity, that it was not *respectful*. This was a reference to the humanistic philosophical position of unconditional positive regard, described within transactional analysis as 'I'm OK, You're OK.' This philosophical perspective is useful because it helps us to be mindful of our more sadistic urges and misanthropic impulses towards others, and assumes a belief in innate human goodness. Naturally I did not want to be understood as someone who does not respect the humanness of the client or patient. However, is there something potentially sadistic in this insistence upon unconditional positive regard, and the OK position, when it subjugates authentic experience? Does taking such a position masquerade as a type of goodness against which others can only then be measured in negative terms? I think the answer to both of these questions is that such a position is in the service of the therapist or supervisor who remains the 'good guy' no matter what (see Davies' discussion, 'Whose Bad Objects Are We Anyway?', 2004). It is captured too by Buber's description of the superiority of the therapist who approaches her patients from the position always of 'I-it' and is never capable of being in the vulnerability and mutual flow and natural imperfection of the 'I-thou' relationship.

Okayness as a manic defence

It seemed that 'Okayness' was being used to disavow feelings, a manifestation of which is an inability to distinguish the symbolic from the concrete. Even though I argued that it was not respectful to deny the shadow side of either ourselves or our clients, that we had a responsibility to reveal these aspects within ourselves and our clients and patients, nothing changed. It became clear that the problem was not a matter of logic but a manic defence (Woods, 2002). How are we to understand the different elements of this manic defence? Was there a fear of owning their vulnerability? Was there a need to view the client as a victim who would be made better through the therapist's diagnosis, use of compassion, empathy and 'understanding'? There is of course a significant amount of literature aimed at viewing the client or patient as an object to be fixed, cured, enabled or healed. This way of thinking endorses the idea that theory is the healing factor in a psychotherapy. Maybe unwittingly some of the psychological literature encourages therapists to idealise their role, leading to an elevation of the therapist and the theory, leaving out the valuable contribution of the client. It is not only the dark forces in our clients and ourselves that we deal with but the shadows in our profession (Guggenbhul Craig, 1971). For instance, I have observed that it can be relatively easy in supervision to steep ourselves in a pathologising frame of mind about our clients and patients, and ignore the positive sides of adversity. In many instances the suffering our clients and patients have endured has motivated them to develop emotional and psychological strength, thinking, for example, of the patient who had been repeatedly subjugated by his father, manipulated by a dominating mother and seriously bullied at school, and yet had gone on to create an ethically sound and extremely successful business, as well as having managed to co-create a satisfying family life. Although internally he was shattered in many ways, of course, part of his recovery was to recognise the gains he had made from his adversities. Unconscious envy of success, affluence, beauty and youth can perhaps sometimes make us exaggerate the negative over the positive as a way of keeping the client or patient as someone dependent on our empathy. In this way we may reinforce their victimhood, implicitly owning our 'superior' power, even though our clients and patients may have talents and gifts greater than us.

Perhaps I was unrealistically disappointed to learn that some therapists who enthusiastically wanted to join the supervision groups defended against knowing themselves more fully through deeper analysis, even when they discovered their lack of resilience. I contrasted this with those clients and patients who have worked through their defences, in many cases traumatic dissociated experiences, yet showed a willingness to travel the painful psychological journey in a way some therapists just refused to do.

We understand defences as a way of protecting more vulnerable parts of self. If a therapist were dissociated from aspects of her shadow self then it would make sense that she would be very anxious when confronted by those aspects in a group situation. In Chapter 2 Brian Fenton refers to his sense of feeling only seen on the 'outside' by the end of his training, at the expense of his subjective reality. Others have expressed feelings such as this. In Chapter 4, Birigitta Heillier recounts her internal crisis which she resolved, not by leaving the supervision group, but by going into deeper analysis.

How to further understand manic defence

In Chapter 5 Sweeting describes the effect of narcissism in the therapist's character, indicating a problem associated with the narcissistic need for perfection, to always feel the 'self love', the superiority of 'goodness' that in varying degrees exists in us all. Maybe this is not just about individual narcissism but also the collective narcissism of a community (Shaw, 2014), who unconsciously use a philosophical perspective to defend against collective dissociated traumatic experiences. As outlined in my chapter on shame, there exists an underlying sense of inferiority often associated with the trauma of loss and disconnection. (See too Heiller's reference to ego psychology as a manic defence against the Holocaust (Aron, 2013) in Chapter 4.) Sweeting describes the needy character of Echo, who is looking for and longing for validity by foregoing her own voice. This is not a dissimilar process to methods observed in cults which rely on the uncritical acceptance of the leader's philosophy and values. Psychological communities, of whatever ilk, are susceptible to this problem, as indeed are most institutions and organisations. Given the very nature of our work with those who have had particularly distorting relational experiences, there is all the more reason for us to resist these tendencies to comply unthinkingly with prevailing orthodoxy. I recall one person, who, although qualified and apparently very experienced, left the group early on because she felt terrified by the authenticity of expression. It seemed that her identity was at stake. Possibly her defence had been strengthened by the type of training she had received, in which the 'objective' was to 'do therapy'.

At the beginning of this journey I expected all therapists to be prepared to share their vulnerability, go to the dark places within them, and stay stable.

Yet we know therapists are injured souls. In a personal communication Cate Masheder, a member of one of the groups, observed that when members of the group had been unable to resolve their injuries enough, or to achieve what Klein refers to as the 'depressive' position (Klein, 1975/1988), the problem cast a shadow over the group process. The shadow side of compassionate, empathic, care-giving role is massive (Guggenbhul Craig, 1971), and debilitating to all clients and patients who are with therapists who will not own their more primitive responses and therefore contain and work with the feelings. I can imagine some people might be thinking, 'But supervision is a developmental process, and you cannot work this way with new therapists.' I can see some truth in this but also take issue with it; it seems to me a view which too easily infantilises trainee psychotherapists. I have worked with relatively new trainees who are psychologically minded enough (of course without the years of knowledge and experience) and with a type of grace and curiosity, a soulfulness, that sustains them in this process. I am thinking here specifically of John (not his real name), a trainee therapist who attended a large group supervision session I led with a colleague. I was slightly nervous for him as I wondered if the bar would be set too high by others in the group who were familiar with the way of working described above. John, though, participated fully and made a significant contribution to the process. He demonstrated humility, eagerness to learn, acknowledgment of his vulnerability and a reflective mind. Do we really need the comfort blankets of 'certainty', to be wrapped around trainee therapists? On the other hand, I have met extremely knowledgeable, 'experienced' therapists who are defensive, and no amount of persuasion works because of the cognitive defence against primitive processes. It seemed that their training had in effect endorsed their defence systems. One might ask in vain, where is the humility, the motivation to be a better therapist? I have come to the conclusion that this is a deeply rooted ethical problem in our profession. After all, whether a trainee or vastly experienced, if a heart surgeon develops an aversion to blood and guts, she will need to have further training, support and at the very least to acknowledge her vulnerability.

In her 1947 essay 'The Ambiguity of Ethics', published in *Les Tempes Moderne*, Simone de Beauvoir argues that when we project power into institutions, systems or people (and we may add to this theory) we subordinate our freedom to think for ourselves and lose our autonomy in what she describes as a type of 'bad faith'. Of course when we no longer project outwards into systems, theories or people we are reliant upon power from within. Naturally this makes us more vulnerable if we are not hiding behind something or someone. *For the relational therapist, her vulnerability is the source of her therapeutic power.*

The bad object

Without paying attention to our deepest, most primitive impulses, without being willing to go through the rubble behind the edifice of our own defence systems, we are left in the vulnerable condition of disavowing our aggression or other 'undesirable' feelings, leaving no space for conflict. If there is no space for aggression, conflict or difference there is a pressure to find unanimity of meaning, so-called harmony, and even perhaps an idealisation of containment.

The concept of the 'bad object' has its roots in Kleinian (1975/1988) theory, and is based on the idea of the infant defending against their anxieties by projecting anxiety, frustration and other negative feelings outward. In the development of a mature ego a person is enabled to integrate both bad and good experiences through the internalisation of a good enough object. When this maturing process has been compromised by varying degrees of trauma, based on abandonment, abuse or, more commonly, cumulative experiences of neglect to our inner subjective world, we are vulnerable to experiencing negative or difficult feelings as overwhelming because we fear they will make us bad, not good enough. We defend ourselves from our 'badness' by projection, leaving us free to feel our 'goodness'. It is only through an intensely affective process that earlier wounds of trauma can be metabolised and tolerated by the conscious mind. This involves a journey into the unknown, as in the previously mentioned 'forest', with a guide whom we can trust, who obviously needs to be a therapist with experience of the 'forest' themselves.

Traditionally humanistic theory has paid little attention to this part of the psyche. Carl Rogers for example focused mostly on the goodness in the client and the process of self-actualisation, which is apparently reached through empathy and congruence. Within TA theory there is a more robust concept known as the 'pig parent' (Steiner, 1974). This part of the psyche has also been described in colourful ways as 'the little fascist' (ibid.) or as a type of electrode. It represents an irrational and destructive part of the self analogous with Klein's 'bad object'. The methodology designed to work with this part of the psyche in traditional TA practice tends to deal with the surface affect of the experience, but not the depth of attachment to trauma sequestered deep within our unconscious.

The leader as the bad object

When the group process involved the expression of primitive self-states such as disgust, hatred, murderous feelings, hostility or indeed anguish or manic hilarity, and when other types of conflict emerged between group members, those therapists, without consciousness of their shadow sides, found it too threatening of their sense of self. At such times I became a target of their unacknowledged aggression: the bad object. This process can be understood from the Kleinian perspective of internalised splitting, as an unconscious defence against their fear or even terror of their own destructive feelings. There was both envy that I could feel these feelings and remain OK with myself (as far as they could see, although I say more about my vulnerabilities below), whilst at the same time a denial of their aggression towards me.

In those early years, I sometimes felt a sense of shame that I had 'gone too far', that I was not behaving professionally or competently enough, feelings which, when analysed, also involved projective identifications from group members (see Chapter 8 on shame). My sense of my own narcissistic need to be seen as a competent supervisor was consistently challenged by this process as I experienced unease at moving away from the more traditional role of the supervisor. Nevertheless I was determined to continue with the process, knowing it would lead to a discovery of deeper layers of relatedness.

Pressure on me

As we traversed these troubled waters I spent time in my analysis and supervision working through the meaning of my disturbance. In analysis, I strengthened my capacity to tolerate and contain varying and contradictory self-states. This meant I began to feel more comfortable with the paradoxical nature of meaning, and more able to resist the demand of some group members to make *sense* of clinical material. I felt my *genuine* competency increase the more conscious I remained of the dialectical nature inherent in difference. I learned to trust that the paradoxical nature of truth is often contained within polarities of feeling and thought. The increased psychological strength gained enabled me to trust my intuitive self as an *involved* participant in group process. This confidence was implicitly passed into the group. Participants felt they too could be powerful and know their own minds in different and varying ways. To support this process theoretically, I made many group interpretations and encouraged relational theorising. For example, the Jungian metaphor of alchemy in which the alchemist (therapist) uses base metal (the darkest part of the psyche) in his search for gold (the discovery of self) provided a professional and anchoring context for the group process. Freeman describes how this theme is common to many myths where the hero from a humble background makes good, which 'is a clear mythologem, namely that which has the lowest value is ultimately that which comes to have the highest' (2014, p. 16). Learning to trust in the alchemical nature of dynamics beyond our immediate cognitive understanding liberated me and the group to play and be creative within an intellectually agreed framework that such a process could be transformative and give birth to new ways of thinking. This is put more poetically by a current member of the group:

> I find the group disturbs the soul through the clients and our own disturbance of everyday life but because of the boundary that has been created there is a freedom
> > to process freely that helps the soul to settle,
> > > settle to see the truth,
> > the truth of the process in those moments,
> > as the truth changes in different situations;
> > and to have open minds to different truths.
> > > > (personal communication, Ghaemrasekh, 2015)

When my psychoanalytic supervisor expressed incredulity at the experience I described, saying he would be too scared to engage in this type of process, I appreciated his honesty, but felt anxious that he seemed to be suggesting I might be rather foolish to work in this way. I had a lonely sense that I was on my own with it. I inferred some criticism from him, maybe a sense that I was being masochistic. In a recent personal communication Carole Shadbolt pointed out that the opposite pole to masochism is surrender, referring to Emanuel Ghent's essay on 'Masochism, Submission and Surrender' (1990), where he makes a distinction between the idea of feeling defeated, as in masochism, and the sense of freedom and liberation that comes from surrender. Borrowing from Ghent's thinking I now understand that I was able to acknowledge my insecurities to myself, not from a feeling of defeat, but as a rational vulnerable experience, and once I had surrendered in this way, I could share my experiences with the group, not as a victim, not to manipulate, but as serious concerns and reflections. This proved to be liberating. It provided an opportunity for the development of the group's reflective capacity as they mused variously and collectively on my thoughts. Through such a process of mutuality and reciprocity we together became more fully conscious of what we were doing, why we were doing it and why it would sometimes feel like a treacherous, rather dangerous journey; indeed we were all liberated through a process of mutual surrender. In sharing my thoughts more explicitly with the group I helped them to see me as a subject, rather than just an object.

> The freedom of no boundaries within the boundaries helps the unconscious to come
> > up to the surface
> > to float
> > and evolves into
> > 'A Language'
> > that becomes meaningful and gives meaning to meaning.
> > (personal communication, Ghaemrasekh, 2015)

My supervisor's second observation was that sometimes I lost a sense of my boundary by becoming too immersed in the process. This useful intervention strengthened my ability to contain and detach, to hold inside me my observing ego, even when immersed in the group processes. My ability to contain, of course, worked its way unconsciously into the groups I was running. As they sensed that holding in me, group members found their own internal vessel, which in turn constellated an archetypal repository within which the whole group, myself included, was contained. This made challenging experiences feel more manageable and therefore more satisfying. The question of whether it was possible to play, improvise, hold and contain what had emerged began to take form.

On learning from the group

In these early years the way the group was set up meant that we all found ourselves to be on a steep learning curve. In the process we were learning a huge amount about ourselves, each other, the effect on supervision and the client case material. Although I often felt fundamentally challenged as I dealt with my own uncertainty (stressing here that I was confident enough to feel the uncertainty) about what I was doing, and the extent to which I carried projective identifications of shame and anxiety that both belonged to me and the group, gradually the value of this way of working began to outweigh these anxieties. Together we learned that by understanding the group process, no matter how disturbing, as a form of communication, and not as a judgement, it would lead to a more deeply satisfying experience. The group became able to distinguish between the easier, quite gratifying way of making 'sense' of everything and the deeper, more satisfying process of finding multiple meanings. Just as I modelled how to trust my intuitive self, so too did members of the group learn to trust their feelings and trust their reflective capacities to contain, and know themselves and others, from a deeper layer of connection within themselves. In Chapter 6 Jane Todd describes how she intuitively used the group, with an informed discussion on gender dynamics. Through her delightful use of metaphors she portrays the unconscious dimension of relational supervision in action.

Supervision as therapy or as therapeutic?

Some members of the group acknowledged that through the relational supervision process they have made significant psychological change, as though in therapy. Much is said about the 'teach/treat' boundary, discussed in Chapters 3 and 4, but for myself, although I have felt invited to be the therapist, I have found it relatively easy (with a few exceptions) to keep the boundary between therapy and supervision. This is partly because the group themselves provide such a competent sense of containment. In this way we all partake in a therapeutic and transformative experience, which does not involve the intrusive nature of 'doing therapy' in a supervisory context. They have changed through this process, as have I; see Marion Umney's interesting account of her personal change and its effect upon her clinical work in Chapter 7, in which she describes how her 'thinking' got in the way of her therapy work. Although in learning to trust more her feelings and reflective capacity, Marion never loses the sharp clarity of her thinking. One of the delights of working in this way is discovering the possibility to work with other *minds*, to create a space where there is a genuine meeting of minds. I have been challenged and changed, and experienced the group as a mutually transforming process. The main advantage of working in this way was revealed by an increasing sense of autonomy and authority within the therapists as they felt more resilient and took ownership of all aspects of themselves. This segued into the effects on clinical work which became more effective and satisfying.

The process I have been through has taught me that therapists who have deep-seated unresolved narcissistic issues cannot work in the *full* sense of relatedness. Without the involvement of the therapist's vulnerability there will be no fundamental change in the therapy.

The ubiquity of transference in the supervisor relationship – ethics

The relational way of working can be deceptive and lead erroneously to a false belief that supervisor and supervisees are equal. Making distinctions between mutuality, reciprocity and equality became quite important as I clarified that, whilst we often had deep connections in the group, whilst I gained enormously from the work we did together, and although I too was changed in the process, *the relationship was still asymmetrical*. This was especially so at times when I needed to be didactic and make challenging statements to a therapist even though the rest of the group disagreed. Two instances spring to mind. One was the presentation by a therapist of a client who was clearly suicidal and breaking the therapeutic boundary by not turning up. I cut across our usual structure when it seemed to be meandering and disavowing of the urgency of the situation by speaking directly to the therapist and telling him to ring the client immediately to come to the therapist's office. It was clear that the overall sense was one of powerlessness, in the client, the therapist and the group; it was as if no one could own any power and there was a sense of us all sleepwalking towards the client's certain death. I noticed how insistent I had to be as a group member challenged me and reprimanded for being 'too harsh', which I think was a thinly veiled objection to my using my power. I had to override her objection, which led to an intense interpersonal discussion about the use of personal authority, power and our moral obligations as supervisors.

Another incident was when the presenter brought a client who was the partner of a jailed convict and paedophile. The issue seemed to be that the client, who had children and grandchildren, wanted to continue a relationship with the man upon his imminent release from jail; the client seemed to be under the sway of the paedophile, unable to think about the potential consequences on her and her family. The group process was inclined towards trying to understand the woman's need and meet her relational need to have this man in her life. Instead I insisted that the therapist tell the woman to own her own power by facing up to her responsibilities towards her children and grandchildren. The group swell seemed to be against such directness and certainty of action.

'Power with' rather than 'power over', as described by Heather Fowlie in Chapter 3, is an ideal to strive for, but cannot be understood outside of the framework of transferential processes. For example in both instances the process could be understood as an attempt to undermine the leader by attacking her power, rather than negotiating with her. When the group, in a process, goes to one side of a polarity then the supervisor has to find a way of introducing the other side of the polarity, and in the process hopefully find the third way. The supervisor is responsible for not allowing herself to be in a confluence of opinion with the group, but to keep a part of her mind on the responsibility to the client. After all relational supervision, with its mutuality and reciprocity, is not the same as peer supervision. The supervisor has to take responsibility for holding the space for the 'moral third' (Benjamin, 2009). In such a situation I needed to find a part of my mind that was separate and mindful of my responsibility to the clients and patients involved, and not to be unnecessarily sensitive about criticism related to using my 'power over' as I demanded, in both cases, that the therapists move away from feeling powerless, and own their authority in the situation. Predictably, the parallel process of my owning my authority and power reverberated in the therapists, which then was positively reflected in the subsequent decisions made by the clients.

In summary

Throughout this book there have been personal, lively accounts of therapists willing to go within themselves, to find the internal world of their clients, to look for the unconscious truths 'that do not always know when or how to speak in words' (personal communication, Ghaemrasekh, 2015) but are revealed through 'disordered language' (ibid.). It takes honesty and courage to deal with the dark forces with which we are presented in clinical situations. It also takes intellectual energy and commitment to bring theoretical understanding to the most nuanced, yet significant of relational processes.

Each author has raised many questions, as have I, about the nature, task and experience of supervision and the power dynamics involved, especially the power of the supervisor to do good or damage. In raising these issues we hope to have provided an opportunity for further reflection on the meaning of supervision, and opened up some controversial areas for discussion.

It is a huge privilege to be a supervisor of psychotherapists who take their work seriously and strive to be competent in their profession. In company with all supervisors, I have attracted diverse transferences, as we all do in this work. I have been variously described by supervisees as warm, passionate, forceful, fiery, gentle, thoughtful, dogmatic, knowledgeable, harsh, critical, compassionate, soulful, loving, insightful and much more. In my understanding of transference, there is always at the very least a grain of truth in it. Sometimes this says as much about the person as me. For example they may see in me something of the hidden life in them, or it may be quite straightforward and in the mutuality of the relationship, in which case I have to own my vulnerability to receive; other times it feels like a shared experience in the intersubjective space, part me, part them. Transference is inevitable. I find the need to deal with it differently as a supervisor from how I deal with it as a therapist, but to my peril do I ignore it! My ideal style of working is to introduce my thoughts, as though another object in the room, as a 'third' in the dynamics, which can be reflected on, thought about, fought with, and give rise to more reflections. This way of naming the 'elephant' in the room allows all of us to negotiate the meaning of this 'elephant', and for me to own what feels really accurate about me. Of course my preferred, ideal style is not always the way it goes, as has been revealed throughout this book.

Thank you for reading. My wish, and our wish, is for you to find, in these pages, inspiration to be as true to yourselves as clinicians and supervisors as you possibly can be, and in that way to offer the best that you can possibly be.

Bibliography

Allen, J.G. and Fonagy, P. (2006). *Handbook of Mentalization-Based Treatment.* Chichester, UK: John Wiley.

Allen, J.R. (2011). 'Relational practices and interventions: neuroscience underpinnings'. In Fowlie, H. and Sills, C. (eds), *Relational Transactional Analysis: Principles in Practice.* London: Karnac Books.

Aron, L. (1990). 'One person and two person psychologies and the method of psychoanalysis'. *Psychoanalytic Psychology*, 7(4):475–85.

Aron, L. (1996). *A Meeting of the Minds: Mutuality in Psychoanalysis.* Hillsdale, NJ: The Analytic Press.

Aron, L. (1999). 'Clinical choices and the relational matrix'. *Psychoanalytic Dialogues*, 9:1–29.

Aron, L. (2006). 'Analytic impasse and the third: Clinical implications of intersubjectivity theory'. *International Journal of Psychoanalysis*, 87:349–68.

Aron, L. (2013). 'Mutual vulnerability: an ethic of clinical practice'. Fourth Annual Conference, International Association of Relational Transactional Analysis. London.

Aron, L. (2014). 'Relational psychotherapy in Europe: A view from across the Atlantic'. In Loewenthal, D. and Samuels, A. (eds). *Relational Psychotherapy, Psychoanalysis and Counselling: Appraisals and Reappraisals.* London and New York: Taylor and Francis.

Aron, L. and Benjamin, J. (1999). 'The development of intersubjectivity and the struggle to think'. Paper presented at the Spring Meeting, Division of Psychoanalysis (39), American Psychological Association. New York, 17 April.

Aron, L. and Harris, A. (2005). 'Introduction'. In Aron, L. and Harris, A. (eds). *Relational Psychoanalysis* (Vol. 2, pp. xiii–xxi). Hillsdale, NJ: The Analytic Press.

Asay, T.P. and Lambert, M.J. (1999). 'The empirical case for the common factors in therapy: Quantitative findings'. In Hubble, M.A., Duncan, B.L. and Miller, S.D. (eds), *The Heart and Soul of Change: What Works in Therapy.* Washington, DC: APA Press.

Atwood, G. and Stolorow, R. (2014/1984). *Structures of Subjectivity: Explorations in Psychoanalytic Phenomenology.* Hillsdale, NJ: The Analytic Press.

Bachelard, G. (1958/1994). *The Poetics of Space.* Boston, MA: Beacon Press.

Balint, M. (1937). 'Early developmental states of the ego'. In *Primary Love and Psychoanalytic Technique.* London: Karnac Books, 1965, pp. 151–64.

Balint, M. (1957). *The Doctor, His Patient and the Illness*. London. Pitman Medical. 2nd edition (1964, reprinted 1986). Edinburgh: Churchill Livingstone.

Bass, A. (2014). 'Supervision and analysis at a crossroad: The development of the analytic therapist. Discussion of papers by Joan Sarnat and Emanuel Berman'. *Psychoanalytic Dialogues*, 24:540–8.

Batts, V.B. (1983). 'Knowing and changing the cultural script component of racism'. *Transactional Analysis Journal*, 13(4):255–7.

Beebe, B. and Lachmannn, F. (2003). 'The relational turn in psychoanalysis: A dyadic systems view from infant research'. *Contemporary Psychoanalysis*, 39(3):379–409.

Beebe, B., Jaffe, J. and Lachmann, F.M. (1992). 'A dyadic systems view of communication'. In Skolnick, N.J. and Warshaw, S.C. (eds), *Relational Psychoanalysis*. Hillsdale, NJ: The Analytic Press.

Benjamin, J. (1988). *The Bonds of Love: Psychoanalysis, Feminism and The Problem of Domination*. New York: Pantheon.

Benjamin, J. (2002a). 'Principles of relational psychoanalysis'. First biannual meeting of the International Association for Relational Psychoanalysis and Psychotherapy: New York.

Benjamin, J. (2002b). 'Relational analysts at work: Sense and sensibility'. Conference held 18–20 January 2002 at the Waldorf-Astoria Hotel in New York City.

Benjamin, J. (2004). 'Beyond doer and done to: An intersubjective view of thirdness'. *Psychoanalytic Quarterly*, 73:5–46.

Benjamin, J. (2007). '*Intersubjectivity, thirdness, and mutual recognition*'. *A talk given at the Institute for Contemporary Psychoanalysis*, Los Angeles, CA.

Benjamin, J. (2009). 'Psychoanalytic controversies: A relational psychoanalysis perspective on the necessity of acknowledging failure in order to restore the facilitating and containing features of the intersubjective relationship (the shared third)'. *International Journal of Psychoanalysis*, 90:441–50.

Berne, E. (1961). *Transactional Analysis in Psychotherapy*. New York: Grove Press.

Berne, E. (1964). *Games People Play*. New York: Grove Press.

Berne, E. (1966/1994). *Principles of Group Treatment*. Menlo Park, CA: Shea Books.

Berne, E. (1972). *What Do You Say After You Say Hello*. New York: Grove Press.

Berne, E. (1977). 'Intuition and ego states: The origins of transactional analysis – A series of papers'. San Francisco, CA: TA Press.

Berne, E. (2001). *The Structure and Dynamics of Organisations and Groups*. Freemantle, Australia: Freemantle Publishing. (Original work published 1963).

Beutler, L.E. and Harwood, T.M. (2002). 'What is and what can be attributed to the therapeutic relationship?' *Journal of Contemporary Psychotherapy*, 32:25–33.

Bion, W.R. (1962). *Learning from Experience*. London: Karnac Books.

Bion, W.R. (1967). *Second Thoughts*. New York: Jason Aronson.

Bion, W.R. (1984). *Second Thoughts: Selected Papers on Psycho-Analysis*. New York: Maresfield Library.

Bollas, C. (1987). *The Shadow of the Object*. New York: Columbia University Press.

Bowlby, J. (1958). 'The nature of the child's tie to his mother'. *International Journal of Psychoanalysis*, 39:350–73.

Boyd, S. and Shadbolt, C. (2011). 'Reflections on a theme of relational supervision'. In Fowlie, H. and Sills, C. (eds), *Relational Transactional Analysis: Principles in Practice*, London: Karnac Books.

Bregman Ehrenberg, D. (2014). Presentation at the 5th Annual Conference of the International Relational Transactional Analysis Association. London, October 2014.

Britton, R. (1989). 'The missing link: Parental sexuality in the Oedipus complex'. In Britton, R., Feldman, M. and O'Shaughnessy, E. (eds), *The Oedipus Complex Today*. London: Karnac Books.

Bromberg, P.M. (1983). 'The mirror and the mask: On narcissism and psychoanalytic growth'. *Contemporary Psychoanalysis*, 19:359–87.

Bromberg. P.M. (1993). 'Shadow and substance: A relational perspective on clinical process'. In Mitchell, S.A. and Aron, L. (eds), *Relational Psychoanalysis: The Emergence of a Tradition*. Hillsdale, NJ: Analytic Press, 1999.

Buber, M. (1970/1923). *I and Thou* (Kaufmann, W.A., trans.). New York: Scribner (original work published 1923).

Buber, M. (1999). *Martin Buber on Psychology and Psychotherapy: Essays, Letters, and Dialogue* (ed. Buber Agassi, J.). New York: Syracuse University Press.

Carroll, L. (1865). *Alice's Adventures in Wonderland*. Penguin.

Carroll, L. (1872). *Through the Looking Glass*. Penguin.

Carroll, M. and Tholstrup, M. (2001). *Integrative Approaches to Supervision*. London: Jessica Kingsley Publishers.

Casement, P. (1985). *On Learning From The Patient*. London: Tavistock Publications Limited.

Cassorla, R.M. (2001). 'Acute enactment as a "resource" in disclosing a collusion between the analytical dyad'. *International Journal of Psychoanalysis*, 82:1155–70.

Cassorla, R.M. (2005). 'From bastion to enactment: The "non-dream" in the theatre of analysis'. *International Journal of Psychoanalysis*, 86:699–719.

Chambers Dictionary, 13th Edition (2014). Chambers Harrap Publishers Ltd.

Chasseguet-Smirgel, J. (1974). Les Chimins de l'anti-Oedipe (Bibliotheque de psychologie clinique). Toulouse: Privat.

Chomsky, N. (1965). *Aspects of a Theory of Syntax*. The Hague: Mouton.

Clarkson, P. (1995). *Change in Organisations*. London: Whurr Publishers.

Cohn, H. (1997). *Existential Thought and Psychotherapeutic Practice*. London: Sage.

Corbett, K. (1996) 'Homosexual boyhood: Notes on girlyboys'. *Gender and Psychoanalysis*, 1:1429–61.

Cornell, W.F. (2015). *Somatic Experience in Psychoanalysis and Psychotherapy*. London and New York: Taylor and Francis.

Cornell, W.F. and Bonds-White, F. (2001). 'Therapeutic relatedness in transactional analysis: The truth of love or the love of truth'. *Transactional Analysis Journal*, 31:71–83.

Cornell, W.F. and Hargaden, H. (eds) (2005). *From Transactions to Relations: The Emergence of a relational tradition in Transactional Analysis*. Chadlington, UK: Haddon Press.

Damasio, A. (1999). *The Feeling of What Happens*. London: Heinemann.

Davies, J.M. (2004). 'Whose bad objects are we, anyway? Repetition and our illusive love affair with evil'. *Psychoanalytic Dialogues*, 14:711–32.

Davies, J.M. and Frawley, M.G. (1994). *Treating the Adult Survivor of Childhood Sexual Abuse*. New York: Basic Books.

de Beauvoir, S. (1947). *The Ethics of Ambiguity*. New York: Citadel.

de Beauvoir, S. (1949/2014). *The Second Sex*. London: Random House.

DeYoung, P. (2003). *Relational Psychotherapy: A Primer*. New York: Brunner-Routledge.

Drego, P. (1983). 'The cultural parent'. *Transactional Analysis Journal*, 13:224–7.

Dworkin, M. (2005). *EMDR and The Relational Imperative*. New York: Routledge.

Eigen, M. (2006a). 'The annihilated self'. *Psychoanalytic Review*, 93(1):25–38.

Eigen, M. (2006b). *Feeling Matters*. London: Karnac Books.

Ekstien, R. (1969). 'Concerning the teaching and learning of psychoanalysis'. *The Journal of the American Psychoanalytic Association*, 17(2):312–32.

Emerson, P. and Frosh, S. (2009). *Critical Narrative Analysis in Psychology. A Guide to Practice*. Basingstoke, UK: Palgrave Macmillan.

Engels, F. (1888). In Hunt, T. (2009). *The Frock Coated Communist: The Life and Times of the Original Champagne Socialist*. London: Penguin.

English, F. (1969). 'Episcripts and the hot potato game'. *Transactional Analysis Bulletin*, 8(32):77–82.

Erskine, R.G. (1988). *Theories of Methods of an Integrative Transactional Analysis*. San Francisco, CA: TA Press.

Erskine, R.G. and Trautmann, R.L. (1996) 'Methods of an integrative psychotherapy'. *Transactional Analysis Journal*, 26(4):316–28.

Erskine, R.G., Moursund, J.P. and Trautmann, R.L. (1999) *Beyond Empathy: A Therapy of Contact-in-Relationship*. Philadelphia, PA: Brunner/Mazel.

Ferenczi, S. (1988) *The Clinical Diary of Sandor Ferenczi*, ed. J. Dupont. Cambridge, MA: Harvard University Press.

Fiscalani, J. (1997). 'On Supervisory parataxis and dialogue'. In M.H. Rock (ed.), *Psychodynamic Supervision*. Northvale, NJ: Jason Aronson, pp. 29–58.

Fonagy, P. (1999). 'The process of change and the change of processes: What can change in a good analysis'. Keynote address to the spring meeting of Division 39 of the American Psychological Association, New York, 16 April 1999.

Fonagy, P. (2003). *Psychoanalytic Theories*. Philadelphia, PA: Whurr Publishers.

Fonagy, P. and Target, M. (1998). 'Mentalization and the changing aims of child psychoanalysis'. *Psychoanalytic Dialogues*, 8:87–114.

Fonagy, P., Gergely, G., Jurist, E. and Target, M. (2004). *Affect Regulation, Mentalization and the Development of the Self*. London: Karnac Books.

Fowlie, H. (2005). 'Confusion and introjection: A model for understanding the defensive structure of the Parent and Child ego states'. *Transactional Analysis Journal*, 35:192–204.

Fowlie, H. and Sills, C. (eds) (2011). 'Introduction'. In *Relational Transactional Analysis, Principles in Practice*. London: Karnac Books, pp. xxv–xxxii.

Frawley-O'Dea, M. (1998). 'Revisiting the "teach/treat" boundary in psychoanalytic supervision: When the supervisee is or is not in current treatment'. *The Journal of the American Academy of Psychoanalysis*, 25:515–27.

Frawley-O'Dea, M.G. (2003). 'Supervision is a relationship too: A contemporary approach to psychoanalytic supervision'. *Psychoanalytic Dialogues*, 13(3):355–66.

Frawley-O'Dea, M. and Sarnat, J.E. (2001). *The Supervisory Relationship*. New York, NY: Guildford Press.

Freeman, D. (2014). 'The stone that the builders rejected'. In Dale Mathers (ed.), *Alchemy and Psychotherapy*. Hove, UK: Routledge.

Freud, S. (1912). *Recommendations for Physicians Practicing Psychoanalysis*. Standard Edition, vol. 12:109–20. London: Hogarth Press.

Freud, S. (1940). 'An outline of psychoanalysis'. In Strachey, J. (ed.) (1964), *Standard Edition of the Complete Psychological Works of Sigmund Freud*, vol. 23. London: Hogarth Press and the Institute of Psycho-Analysis.

Gabbard, G.O. (1992). 'Commentary on "dissociative processes and transference-countertransference paradigms" by Jody Messler Davies and Mary Gale Frawley'. *Psychoanalytic Dialogues*, 2:37–47.

Gabbard, G.O. and Wilkinson, S.M. (1994). *Management of Countertransference with Borderline Patients*. Lanham, MD: Jason Aronson.

Geertz, C. (1973). *The Interpretation of Cultures: Selected Essays*. New York: Basic Books.

Gerson, S. (2008). 'Unconscious phantasy and relational reality'. *Psychoanalytic Inquiry*, 28:151–68.

Gerson, S. (2009). 'When the third is dead: memory, mourning, and witnessing in the aftermath of the Holocaust'. *International Journal of Psychoanalysis*, 90:1341–57.

Ghaemrasekh, F. (2015). Personal communication.

Ghent, E. (1990). 'Masochism, submission, surrender: Masochism as a perversion of surrender'. *Contemporary Psychoanalysis*, 26:108–36.

Gill, M.M. (1987). The analyst as participant. *Psychoanalytic Inquiry*, 7:249–60.

Gill, M.M. (1994a). 'Heinz Kohut's self psychology'. In Goldberg, A. (ed.), *A Decade of Progress: Progress in Self Psychology*, Vol. 10, Hillsdale, NJ: The Analytic Press, pp. 97–211.

Gill, M.M. (1994b). *Psychoanalysis in Transition*. Hillsdale, NJ: The Analytic Press.

Goulding, R. and Goulding, M. (1978). *The Power is in the Patient: A TA/Gestalt Approach to Psychotherapy*. San Francisco, CA: TA Press.

Green, A. (1986). *On Private Madness*. London: Karnac Books.

Green, A. (2001). 'The dead mother'. In Green, A. (trans. A. Weller), *Life Narcissism and Death Narcissism*. London: Free Association Books.

Greene, L. and Sharman-Burke, J. (2000). *The Mythic Journey. The Meaning of Myth as a Guide for Life*. New York: Fireside.

Guggenbuhl-Craig, A. (1971). *Power in the Helping Professions*. Woodstock, CT: Spring Publications Inc.

Hadley, M. (2008). 'Relational theory'. In Berzoff, J., Melano-Flanagan, L. and Hertz, P. (eds), *Inside Out and Outside In* (2nd edn.). New York: Jason Aronson, pp. 205–28

Hargaden, H. (2010). 'When parting is not such sweet sorrow in life scripts'. In Erskine, R., (ed.) *Analysis of Unconscious Relational Patterns*. London: Karnac Books, pp. 55–71.

Hargaden, H. (2013a). 'Response to Jacobs-Wallfisch's "Wounds of History"'. Paper presented in December 2013, to Conference entitled 'Intergenerational Trauma' at the Tavistock Centre, London.

Hargaden, H. (2013b). 'You don't need to make it look as though you were never here'. Paper presented in December 2013, to Conference entitled 'Intergenerational Trauma' at the Tavistock Centre, London.

Hargaden, H. (2014a). 'Building resilience: The role of firm boundaries and the third in relational group therapy'. *Transactional Analysis Journal*. Sage. DOI: 10.1177/0362153713515178.

Hargaden, H. (2014b). 'Relational as theory? Relational as a principle? Relational as symbol of integration?'. In Loewenthal, D. and Samuels, A. (eds), *Relational Psychotherapy, Psychoanalysis and Counselling*. London and New York: Taylor and Francis.

Hargaden, H. and Fenton, B. (2005) 'An analysis of nonverbal transactions drawing on theories of intersubjectivity'. *Transactional Analysis Journal*, 35(2):173–86.

Hargaden, H. and Schwartz, J. (2007). Editorial. *European Journal of Psychotherapy and Counselling*, 9(1):3–5.

Hargaden, H. and Sills, C. (2002). *Transactional Analysis: A Relational Perspective*. London: Brunner-Routledge.

Hauser, M.D. (2006). *Moral Minds*. New York: HarperCollins.

Hawkins, P. and Shohet, R. (1989). *Supervising in the Helping Professions*. Milton Keynes: Open University Press.

Heathcote, A. (2010). 'Eric Berne's Development of Ego State Theory: Where did it all begin and who influenced him?'. *Transactional Analysis Journal*, 40(3–4):254–60.

Heaton, J. and Groves, J. (1994). *Introducing Wittgenstein*. Royston, UK: Pub Iconbooks Ltd.

Hegel, G.W.F. (1874). *'The Logic': Encyclopaedia of the Philosophical Sciences*. 2nd Edition. London: Oxford University Press.

Heiller, B. and Sills, C. (2010). 'Life Scripts: An Existential Perspective'. In Erskine, R. (ed.), *Life Scripts – A Transactional Analysis of Unconscious Relational Patterns*. London: Karnac Books.

Heiman, P. (1940). The analyst's responses to the patient paper delivered to the 16th International Psychoanalytic Congress. Zurich.

Heller, M.D. (2010). 'Working in psychological space part II: Using the intersubjective field to access, decode and understand what lies beneath'. *The Therapist Magazine*, online edition May–June 2010.

Herman, J.L. (1992). *Trauma and Recovery*. London: Pandora.

Hine, J. (1990). 'The bilateral and ongoing nature of games'. *Transactional Analysis Journal*, 20(1):28–39.

Hoffman, I.Z. (1998). 'Ritual and spontaneity in the psychoanalytical process. A dialectical- constructivist view'. Hillsdale, NJ: The Analytic Press.

Holloway, E. (1995). *Clinical Supervision: A Systems Approach.* London: Sage Publications.

Holloway, E. and Wolleat, P. (1994). 'Supervision: The pragmatics of empowerment'. *Journal of Educational and Psychological Consultation*, 5(1).

Hunt, J. (2008). IARTA booklet, www.relationalta.com.

Jacobs-Wallfisch, M. (2013). 'The wounds of history'. A paper presented in December 2013 to Conference entitled 'Intergenerational Trauma' at the Tavistock Centre, London.

Jacoby, M. (1994). *Shame: Origins of Self Esteem.* London: Routledge.

Johnson, S. (1994). *Character Styles.* New York: W.W. Norton and Company.

Joseph, B. (1989). *Psychic Equilibrium and Psychic Change.* London and New York: Routledge.

Jung, C.G. (1990). *The Archetypes and the Collective Unconscious*, vol. 9, part 1. London: Routledge.

Kahler, T. (1975). 'Drivers: The key to the process script'. *Transactional Analysis Journal*, 5(3):280–4.

Karpman, S. (1968). 'Fairy tales and script drama analysis'. *Transactional Analysis Bulletin.* 7(26):39–43.

Keats, J. (1899). *The Complete Poetical Works and Letters of John Keats.* Cambridge Edition. Houghton Mifflin.

Kilborn, B. (2002). *Disappearing Persons.* Albany, NY: State University of New York Press.

Klein, M. (1932). *The Psycho-Analysis of Children.* London: Hogarth Press.

Klein, M. (1946). 'Notes on Some Schizoid Mechanisms'. *International Journal of Psycho-analysis*, 27:99–110.

Klein, M. (1959). 'Our adult world and its roots in infancy'. In Klein, M. (1993) *Collected Works, vol. 111, Envy and Gratitude and Other Works.* London: Karnac Books.

Klein, M. (1975/1988). *Envy and Gratitude and other works 1946–1963.* London: Virago Books.

Kohut, H. (1971). *The Analysis of the Self.* New York: International Universities Press.

Kohut, H. and Wolf, E.S. (1978). 'The disorders of the self and their treatment: An outline'. *International Journal of Psychoanalysis*, 59:413–25.

Kondo, D. (1990). *Crafting Selves; Power, Gender and Discources of Identity in a Japanese Workplace.* Chicago, IL: University of Chicago Press.

Kovács, V. (1935). 'Lehranalyse und kontrollanalyse'. *Internationale Zeitschrift für Psychoanalyse.* XXI Band, Heft 4.

Lacan, J. (1977). *Ecrits, a Selection.* Sheridan, A. (trans.). New York: Norton.

Lambert, M.J. and Ogles, B.M. (2004). 'The efficacy and effectiveness of psychotherapy'. In Lambert Bergin, M.J. (ed.), *Garfield's Handbook of Psychotherapy and Behaviour Change* (5th edn.). New York: Wiley.

Lasch, C. (1979). *The Culture of Narcissism.* London: Abacus.

Lee, L. (2008). IARTA booklet, www.relationalta.com.

Levi Strauss, C. (1967). *Les structures élèmentaires de la parente*, Paris: Presses Universitaires de France.

Levine, P.A. (2010). *In an Unspoken Voice: How the Body Releases Trauma and Restores Goodness*. Berkeley, CA: North Atlantic Books.

Little, M. (1951). 'Countertransference and the patient's response to it'. *International Journal of Psychoanalysis*, 32:32–40.

Little, R. (2001). 'Schizoid processes: Working with the defences of the withdrawn child ego state'. *Transactional Analysis Journal*, 31(1):33–43.

Little, R. (2004). 'Ego state relational units and resistance to change: An integration of transactional analysis & object relations'. *Transactions: The Journal of the Institute of Transactional Analysis*, 1:3–10.

Little, R. (2006). 'Relational transactional analysis: The therapist's stance'. *The Script*, 36(3). International Transactional Analysis Association.

Little, R. (2011). 'Countertransference self-disclosure'. In Fowlie, H. and Sills, C. (eds), *Relational Transactional Analysis. Principles in Practice*. London: Karnac Books.

Little, R. (2012). 'The inevitability of unconscious engagements and the desire to avoid them: A commentary on Stuthridge'. *Transactional Analysis Journal*, 42(4):257–64.

Little, R. (2013). 'The new emerges out of the old: An integrated relational perspective on psychological development, psychopathology, and therapeutic action'. *Transactional Analysis Journal*, 43(2):106–21.

Loewald, H. (1977). 'Primary process, secondary process and language'. In *Papers on Psychoanalysis*. New Haven, CT: Yale University Press, 1980, pp. 178–418.

Loewenthal, D. (2014). 'Relational ethics: From existentialism to post-existentialism'. In Loewenthal, D. and Samuels, A. (eds), *Relational Psychotherapy, Psychoanalysis and Counselling: Appraisals and Reappraisals*. London and New York: Taylor and Francis.

Loewenthal, D. and Samuels, A. (2014). *Relational Psychotherapy, Psychoanalysis and Counselling. Appraisals and Reappraisals*. London and New York: Taylor and Francis.

Luborsky, L. and Auerbach, A. (1985). 'The therapeutic relationship in psychodynamic psychotherapy: The research evidence and its meaning for practice'. In Hales, R. and Frances, A. (eds), *Psychiatry update: The American Psychiatric Association Annual Review*. 4:550–61. Washington, DC: American Psychiatric Press.

Lussier, A. (1999). *The Dead Mother Variations on a Theme*. London: Routledge.

Lynch, W. (1712). 'The making of a slave'. Sourced by finalcall.com news last updated 22 May 2009.

McLaughlin, J.T. (2005). *The Healer's Bent: Solitude and Dialogue in the Clinical Encounter*. Northvale, NJ: The Analytic Press.

Maroda, K.J. (2004) *The Power of Countertransference*. Hillsdale, NJ: The Analytic Press.

Marx, K. (1873). *Capital, Vol 1*. Afterword to the Second German Edition (4).

Masterson, J.F. (1988). *The Search for the Real Self*. New York: The Free Press.

Masterson, J.F. and Lieberman, A.R. (2004). *A Therapist's Guide to the Personality Disorders: The Masterson Approach*. Phoenix, AZ: Zeig, Tucker & Theisen, Inc.

May, R. (1991). *The Cry for Myth*. London: Souvenir Press.

Meier, C.A. (1995). *Personality*. Einsiedeln, Switzerland: Daimon. (Original work published 1977).

Mellor, K. (1980). 'Impasses: A developmental and structural understanding'. *Transactional Analysis Journal*, 10(3):213–20.

Mendelsohn, R. (2012). 'Parallel process and projective identification in psychoanalytic supervision'. *Psychoanalytic Review*, 99(3):297–314.

Miehls, D. (2010). 'Contemporary trends in supervision theory: A shift from parallel process to relational and trauma theory'. *Clinical Social Work Journal*, 38:370–8.

Minikin, K. (2011). 'Transactional analysis and the wider world: the politics and psychology of alienation'. In Fowlie, H. and Sills, C. (eds), *Relational Transactional Analysis, Principles in Practice*, pp. xxv–xxxii.

Mitchell, S.A. (1993). *Hope and Dread in Psychoanalysis*. New York: Basic Books.

Mitchell, S.A. (2000). *Relationality: From Attachment to Intersubjectivity*. New York: The Analytic Press.

Mitchell, S.A. (2002). *Can Love Last? The Fate of Romance Over Time*. New York: Norton.

Mitchell, S.A. and Aron, L. (1999). *Relational Psychoanalysis. The Emergence of a Tradition*. Hillsdale, NJ: The Analytic Press.

Modell, A.H. (1999) 'The dead mother syndrome and the reconstruction of trauma'. In G. Kohen (ed.), *The Dead Mother: The Work of André Green*. New York: Routledge.

Moiso, C. (1985). 'Ego states and transference'. *Transactional Analysis Journal*, 15(3):194–201.

Moiso, C. and Novellino, M. (2000). 'An overview of the psychodynamic school of transactional analysis and its epistemological foundations'. *Transactional Analysis Journal*, 30(3):182–91

Mollon, P. (2001). *Releasing the Self: The healing legacy of Heinz Kohut*. London: Whurr Publishers.

Mollon, P. (2008). *Psychoanalytic Energy Psychotherapy*. London: Karnac Books.

Montross, C. (2013). *Falling Into the Fire: A Psychiatrist's Encounters with the Mind in Crisis*. Penguin Books.

Morrison, A.P. (1994). 'The breath and boundaries of a self-psychological immersion in shame: A one-and-a-half-person psychology'. *Psychoanalytic Dialogues*, 4:19–35.

Morrison, V. (1983). 'Inarticulate speech of the heart'. Polydor, 839604-2. Instrumental and song.

Nitzun, M. (1996). *The Anti Group: Destructive Forces in the Group and their Creative Potential*. New York: Routledge.

Novellino, M. and Moiso, C. (1990). 'The psychodynamic approach to transactional analysis'. *Transactional Analysis Journal*, 20(3):187–92.

Ogden, P. and Minton, K. (2008). *Trauma and the Body: A Sensorimotor Approach to Psychotherapy*. New York: Norton.

Ogden, T.H. (1982/1992). *Projective Identification and Psychoanalytic and Psychotherapeutic Technique*. London: Karnac Books.

Ogden, T.H. (1994). 'The analytic third: Working with intersubjective clinical facts', in Mitchell, S.A. and Aron, L. (1999). *Relational Psychoanalysis. The Emergence of a Tradition*. Hillsdale, NJ: The Analytic Press.

Ogden, T.H. (1982/1992). *Projective identification and Psychotherapeutic Technique.* London: Karnac Books.

Ogden, T. (2004). 'The analytic third: Implications for psychoanalytic theory and technique'. *Psychoanalytic Quarterly*, 72:167–96.

Ogden, T. (2005). 'On psychoanalytic supervision'. *Int. J. Psychoanal.*, 86 (5):1265–80.

O'Loughlin, M. (2009). *The Subject of Childhood.* New York: Peter Lang Publishing Inc.

Orange, D. (2010). *Thinking for Clinicians: Philosophical Resources for Contemporary Psychoanalysis and the Humanistic Psychotherapies.* London: Routledge.

Petriglieri, G. (2007). Welcome address. International Transactional Analysis Conference, San Francisco, CA.

Pines, M. (1994). 'Borderline phenomena in analytical groups'. In Pines, M. (ed.), *Ring of Fire; Primitive Affects in Group Psychotherapy.* London: Routledge.

Proctor, B. (1986). 'Supervision: A co-operative exercise in accountability'. In Marken, M. and Payne, M. (eds), *Enabling and Ensuring: Supervision in practice.* National Youth Bureau, Council for Education and Training in Youth and Community Work. Leicester, UK.

Racker, H. (1968). *Transference and Countertransference.* Madison, CT: International Universities Press.

Rogers, A. (2006). *The Unsayable.* New York: Ballantine Books.

Rogers, C.R. (1951). *Client-Centred Therapy.* London: Constable.

Rogers, C.R. (1970). *Carl Rogers on Encounter Groups.* New York: Harper & Row.

Rogers, C.R. (1996). *A Way of Being.* Orlando, FL: Houghton Mifflin.

Rothschild, B. (2000). *The Body Remembers.* New York: Norton Press.

Samuels, A. (1993). *The Political Psyche.* London and New York: Routledge.

Samuels, A. (2014). 'Shadows of the therapy relationship'. In Loewenthal, D. and Samuels, A. (eds), *Relational Psychotherapy, Psychoanalysis and Counselling: Appraisals and Reappraisals.* London and New York: Routledge.

Sandler, J. (1979). 'Countertransference and Role-Responsiveness'. *International Review of Psycho-Analysis*, 3:43–7.

Sandler, J. (1993). 'On communication from patient to analyst: not everything is projective identification'. *International Journal of Psychoanalysis*, 74:1097–107.

Sarnat, J. (2014). 'Disruption and working through in the supervisory process: A vignette from supervision of a psychoanalytic candidate'. *Psychoanalytic Dialogues*, 24:532–9.

Scharness, G. (2006). 'Transference enactments in clinical supervision'. *Clinical Social Work Journal*, 34(1):407–25.

Schore, A.N. (1994). *Affect Regulation and the Origin of the Self.* New Jersey, NJ: Lawrence Erlbaum Associates.

Schore, A.N. (2000). *'Minds in the making'.* Seventh Annual John Bowlby Memorial Lecture, Centre for Attachment-Based Psychoanalytic Psychotherapy (CAPP) London.

Schore, A.N. (2003/2012). *Affect Regulation and the Repair of the Self.* London: W.W. Norton.

Searles, H.F. (1955). 'The informational value of the supervisor's emotional experiences'. *Journal for the Study of Interpersonal Processes*, 18:135–46.

Shapiro, F. (ed.) (2002). *EMDR as Integrative Psychotherapy: Experts of Diverse Orientation Explore the Paradigm Prism*. Washington, DC: American Psychological Press.

Shadbolt, C. (2009). 'Sexuality and shame'. *Transactional Analysis Journal*, 39(2):163–72.

Shaw, D. (2014). *Traumatic Narcissism*. New York: Routledge.

Shmukler, D. (1991). 'Transference and transactions: Perspectives from developmental theory, object relations, and transformational process'. *Transactional Analysis Journal*, 21(3):127–35.

Silverman, D.K. (1996). 'Arithmetic of a one- and two-person psychology: Merton Gill, an essay'. *Psychoanalytic Psychology*, 13:267–74.

Slavin, J. (1998). 'Influence and vulnerability in psychoanalytic supervision and treatment'. *Psychoanalytic Psychology*, 15(2):230–44.

Sletvold, J. (2014). *The Embodied Analyst. From Freud and Reich to relationality*. London and New York: Routledge.

Solomon, C. (2010). 'Eric Berne the therapist: One patient's perspective'. *Transactional Analysis Journal*, 40(3–4):183–6.

Stark, M. (1998). 'When the body meets the mind: What body psychotherapy can learn from psychoanalysis'. Panel presentation at the First National Conference of the United States Association for Body Psychotherapy.

Stark, M. (1999). *Modes of Therapeutic Action: Enhancement of Knowledge, Provision of Experience and Engagement in Relationship*. Northvale, NJ: Jason Aronson.

Steiner, C. (1974). *Scripts People Live*. New York: Grove Press.

Steiner, C. (2003). 'Core concepts of a stroke-centred transactional analysis'. *Transactional Analysis Journal*, 33(2):178–81.

Stern, D.B. (2003). *Unformulated Experience, from Dissociation to Imagination*. Hillsdale, NJ: The Analytic Press.

Stern, D.B. (2004). 'The eye that sees itself: Dissociation, enactment, and the achievement of conflict'. *Contemporary Psychoanalysis*, 14:197–237.

Stern, D.N. (1985). *The Interpersonal World of the Infant: A View from Psychoanalysis and Developmental Psychology*. New York: Basic Books.

Stern, D.N., Sander, L., Nahum, J., Harrison, A., Lyons-Ruth, K., Morgan, A., Bruschweiler-Stern, N. and Tronick, E. (1998). 'Non-interpretive mechanisms in psychoanalytic therapy: The "something more" than interpretation'. *International Journal of Psychoanalysis*, 79:903–21.

Stolorow, R.D. and Atwood, G.E. (1989). 'The unconscious and unconscious fantasy: An intersubjective-developmental perspective'. *Psychoanalytic Inquiry*, 9:364–74.

Stolorow, R.D. and Atwood, G.E. (1992). *Contexts of Being: The Intersubjective Foundations of Psychological Life*. Hillsdale, NJ: Analytic Press.

Stroll, A. (2002). *Wittgenstein*. Oxford: One World Publications.

Stuthridge, J. (2011). 'What do I do now? Grappling with uncertainty in a postmodern world'. In Fowlie, H. and Sills, C. (eds), *Relational Transactional Analysis. Principles in Practice*. London: Karnac Books.

Stuthridge, J. (2012). 'Traversing the fault lines: Trauma and enactment'. *Transactional Analysis Journal*, 42(4):238–51.

Stuthridge, J. (2015). 'All the world's a stage: Games, enactments and countertransference'. *Transactional Analysis Journal*, 45(2):104–16.

Summers, G. and Tudor, K. (2000). 'Cocreative transactional analysis'. *Transactional Analysis Journal*, 30:23–40.

Symington, N. (1983). 'The analyst's act of freedom as agent of therapeutic change'. *International Journal of Psychoanalysis*, 10:283–91.

Symington, N. (1990). 'The possibility of human freedom and its transmission'. *International Journal of Psychoanalysis*, 71:95–106.

Trevarthen, C. (1979). 'Communication and co-operation in early infancy. A description of primary intersubjectivity'. In Bullara, M. (ed.), *Before Speech:The Beginning of Human Communication*. London: Cambridge University Press.

Trevarthen, C. (1993). 'The functions of emotions in early infant communication and development'. In Nadel, J. and Camioni, L. (eds), *New Perspectives in Early Communicative Development*. London: Routledge.

Tudor, K. and Hargaden, H. (2002). 'The couch and the ballot box: The contribution and potential of psychotherapy in enhancing citizenship'. In Feltham, C. (ed.), *What's the Good of Counselling and Psychotherapy? The Benefits Explained*. London, UK: Sage, pp. 156–78.

Tudor, K. and Summers, G. (2014). *Co-creative Transactional Analysis: Papers, responses, dialogues and developments*. London: Karnac Books.

Van Deurzen, E. and Arnold-Baker, C. (eds) (2005). *Existential Perspectives on Human Issues: A Handbook for Therapeutic Practice*. Basingstoke, UK: Palgrave MacMillan.

Vygotsky, L.S. (1962). *Thought and language* (Hanfmann, E. and Vakar, G. eds and trans.). Cambridge, MA: MIT Press.

Vygotsky, L.S. (1988). 'The genesis of higher mental functions'. In Richardson, K. and Sheldon, S. (eds), *Cognitive Development to Adolescence*. Hove, UK: Erlbaum Associates.

Vygotsky, L.S. (1993). *The collected works of L.S. Vygotsky*, Vol. 2. *The Fundamentals of Defectology* (Abnormal Psychology and Learning Disabilities). Reiber, R. and Carton, A. (eds). New York: Plenum Press.

Wachtel, P.L. (2008). *Relational Theory and the Practice of Psychotherapy*. New York: Guildford Press.

Winnicott, D.W. (1949). 'Hate in the countertransference'. *International Journal of Psychoanalysis*, 30:69–74.

Winnicott, D.W. (1953). 'Transitional objects and transitional phenomena' in *Playing and Reality*. London: Tavistock Publications, 1971.

Winnicot, D.W. (1965). *The Maturational Process and the Facilitating Environment: Studies in the Theory of Emotional Development*. New York: International Universities Press.

Winnicott, D.W. (1968). *The Use of an Object and Relating Through Identification*. Cambridge, MA: Harvard University Press.

Winnicott, D.W. (1971). *Playing and Reality*. London: Tavistock.

Winnicott, D.W. (1975/1945) 'Primitive emotional development'. In *Collected Papers: Through Paediatrics to Psychoanalysis* (Original work published 1945). New York: Basic Books.

Winnicott, D.W. (1985). *The Maturational Processes and the Facilitating Environment*. London: Hogarth Press.

Wittgenstein, L. (1980). 'The Oxford Companion to Philosophy: language-game'. In Baker, G.P. and Hacker, P.M.S., *Analytical Commentary on Philosophical Investigations, Vol. 1: Wittgenstein: Understanding and Meaning*. Oxford: Basil Blackwell, pp. 88–9.

Woods, K. (2002). 'Primary and secondary gains from games'. *Transactional Analysis Journal*, 32(3):190–2.

Yalom, I.D. (1980). *Existential Psychotherapy*. New York: Basic Books.

Yalom, I.D. (1989). *Love's Executioner, and Other Tales of Psychotherapy*, 6th edn. New York, NY: Harper Perennial.

Yalom, I.D. (2002). *The Gift of Therapy*. New York: HarperCollins.

Yellin, J. (2014). 'Miles to go? Towards relational supervision'. *Attachment, New Directions in Psychotherapy and Relational Psychoanalysis*, 8(3):262–80.

Yontef, G. (1988). *Awareness, Dialogue and Process: Essays on Gestalt Therapy*. Gouldsboro, ME: Gestalt Journal Press.

Zhou, K. (2007). *A Basic Mencius: The Wisdom and Advice of China's Second Sage*. San Francisco, CA: Long River Press.

Zinn, J.K. and Nhat Hanh, T. (2009). *Full Catastrophe Living: Using the Wisdom of Your Body and Mind to Face Stress, Pain and Illness*, revised edn. New York, NY: Random House.

Index